Money for Nothing and your Cheques for Free

How banks process payments from small transactions on your mobile to billion-dollar international transfers

Book 1 of The Complete Banker series

By Chris Skinner

The
**Complete
Banker**

First published 2010 by Balatro Limited, 98 Westbury Lane, Buckhursthill, IG9 5PW, UK

ISBN 978-1-907720-06-2

Edited and produced by Searching Finance Ltd, 8 Whitehall Road, London W7 2JE, UK. Tel: +44 (0) 7885 441682; email: enquiries@searchingfinance.co.uk; web: www.searchingfinance.co.uk

Editor: Ann Tierney

Typeset by Deirdré Gyenes

Money for Nothing and your Cheques for Free

How banks process payments from small transactions on your mobile to billion-dollar international transfers

Book 1 of The Complete Banker series

By Chris Skinner

The
**Complete
Banker**

About Chris Skinner

Chris has been providing independent, expert commentary on the key developments in banking for over a decade in his role as Chief Executive of Balatro and Chairman of the Financial Services Club. In particular, he has been writing for various media, such as *The Banker* Magazine, since 2004 and is a key commentator on banking for prime time news channels including the BBC, Sky and Bloomberg. Prior to creating his independent entities, Chris had key roles at management and board levels covering insurance, retail and investment banking across a range of consulting and technology firms.

Chris Skinner has worked worldwide delivering advice, keynote speeches, presentations and workshops to many banks and vendors worldwide, including Accenture, American Express, ANZ, Bank of America, Bank of Baroda, Cisco, Hewlett Packard, Liberty Bank, Lloyds TSB, McKinsey, Merrill Lynch, Microsoft, National Australia Bank, Nationwide Building Society, NCR, TATA, the National Bank of Kuwait, the Union Bank of the Philippines, Wachovia Bank, Washington Mutual, and many others.

About the Financial Services Club

The Financial Services Club is a unique service aimed at senior executives and decision makers from banks, insurance companies, technology firms, consultancies ... in fact, any firm that is interested in understanding and planning for the future operating environment for the financial services markets.

The Financial Services Club bridges the gap between today and tomorrow. It allows you to network with hundreds of professionals all sharing a common interest in the future of the industry. The Club hosts over 50 events a year, in a number of different European countries, with keynote speakers and luminaries from the industry airing their views on the future of financial services. Our illustrious speaker list is targeted to cover all aspects of the industry from practitioners to legislators to futurists.

For more information, go to http://www.fsclub.co.uk

Contents

Preface
Chapter 1: Payments innovation: the new frontiers

Introduction 4

Payments in the cloud (2009) 4

Innovation in payments (Part 1) (2009) 7

Innovation in payments (Part 2) (2009) 11

Payment innovation (Part 3) (2009) 15

A real-time global pulse (2009) 17

Fragmented payments in a connected world (2008) 20

Payments: the next generation (2006) 23

    Major headlines from this report 24

    Payments in a networked world 25

    Micropayments 26

    Contactless payments 28

    Mobile payments 30

    Biometric payments 31

    Payments: the Next Generation 34

    Invisible payments 35

    How would it work? 37

    The future of payments 39

Chapter 2: Mobile payments: a vision of the future

Introduction 42

Mobile payments: the battleground of the future (2009) 42

    Mobile payments: the battle for the future 42

Money for Nothing and your Cheques for Free

Battleground and key protagonists.......................................**43**

A business worth fighting for...**44**

MNO-led models..**45**

Bank-led models..**46**

Corporate mobile payments in bank-led models **47**

Partnership models: a Third Way...**48**

Blueprint for the future..**50**

Conclusions...**51**

Mobile money numbers (2009)...**51**

More about mobile money (2009)...**53**

First O2-RBS Visa Cards, now Nokia Obopay Money
(2009)...**54**

Mobile payments in China (2009)...**55**

Mobile payment provider 'infuriates' banks (2009)..............**56**

M-billing: a killer app? (2008) **58**

Chapter 3: The Paypal story

Introduction..**62**

Why PayPal et al REALLY matter! (2010)..............................**62**

Why PayPal et al don't matter (2010)......................................**66**

PayPal does have competition (2009) **69**

PayPal not so pally (2009)...**70**

PayPal's 10th anniversary (2008)...**72**

Celebrating PayPal's Centenary (2007)....................................**75**

Why PayPal works..**76**

PayPal in Europe..**78**

PayPal Mobile **79**

Why bankers don't get it...**81**

PayPal's future **83**

Chapter 4: Remittances: where the money's at

Introduction 86

Remittances and the need for financial inclusion (2010)...... 86

More on remittances (2010) 91

Why banks should avoid the remittance market (2010) 92

Escape with Phones4U (2009) 96

More on remittances (2009).. 97

A remittance strategy scribble (2009) 99

Remittances numbers (2009).. 103

Chapter 5: Regulation: from SEPA to PSD, and beyond

Introduction 108

What happens to SEPA, Chi-x etc if the euro fails? (2010)... 108

A new PSD-approved Payments Institution starts business
(2010) 114

This house believes that SEPA does matter ... or does it?
(2010) 117

Are you taking the PSD? (2010)................................... 120

40 days of the PSD (2009) 122

    What is the PSD? 125

    Short-term issues with the PSD 126

    Full amount principle and charging options 127

More on the SEPA DD launch (2009) 128

Today is SEPA day, wa-hey! (2009) 130

PSD and SEPA research results (2009) 134

    European payments: a land of confusion 134

    Key findings... 137

    Conclusions.. 140

Money for Nothing and your Cheques for Free

The total view on SEPA and the PSD (2009) 141

    SEPA implementation 143

    PSD implementation 146

    Corporates and SEPA 148

Quantifying people's views on SEPA (2009) 149

The danger that SEPA may not happen (2009) 152

SEPA and the PSD aren't broken ... just irrelevant (2009) ... 158

So what is the cost benefit of SEPA? (2007) 161

Chapter 6: Fraud and security matters

Introduction 168

Why identity management is so complicated (2010) 168

Chip & PIN is broken (2010) 172

Eye, eye – the future of customer identity? (2010) 174

Forget payments, think value (2009) 177

We know who you are ... or do we? (2009) 180

How many cards are left in chip & PIN terminals every day?

(2008) 183

This house believes our authentication and identification

methods work (2008) 185

PINs and passwords: useful or useless? (2008) 187

Chip and PIN five years from now (2009) 197

Preface

I've spent my life around money. Not making any, but watching how it's processed, managed and organised. This privilege has been afforded to me by working for some of the largest technology firms providing payments processing systems.

Working with banks on their payments systems, you realise how critical these systems are to our world of commerce and society today. You could not be reading this book without payments systems working. You could not make a phone call, get a newspaper, drink a Coke or do anything without payments and efficient payments processing.

You see, payments is money and there's not much you can do without money these days apart from breathing and walking ... and some governments even want to tax that!

Hence, if you think that money is important, then so is the ability to process money: payments.

And that's what this book is all about: from processing payments over the internet and on your mobile telephone; to payments via cards, cash and cheques; to massive international payments operations and the challenges faced by banks in these areas to avoid money launderers and terrorists.

I find it all incredibly interesting, but then I am a nerdy-nerd when it comes to money.

Hopefully, I won't turn you into a nerdy-nerd but if you have the slightest interest in money and banking, then you'll find this a useful addition to your bookshelf, I'm sure.

Meantime, if you want to become a complete banker, then keep adding our small works of observations about the industry to your

Money for Nothing and your Cheques for Free

knowledge as we add to this, the first in our series of books about banking in the Complete Banker series.

Have fun and enjoy the read,

Chris

PS: The articles herein have been selected from white papers, presentations and other research I have undertaken, and from my regular Financial Services Club blog postings; at http://www.thefinanser.com for more information on the Financial Services Club, go to http://www.fsclub.co.uk

Chapter 1 Payments innovation: the new frontiers

Introduction

Payments innovation is a tough call for banks. This is because payments should be safe and risk-free. Innovation in payments implies change and change implies risks. This is why banks don't change their payments engines too often. Having said that, there is some innovation in payments, especially in the retail payments space where mobile and contactless transactions have really taken off in recent years. So where are the new frontiers in payments? Let's have a look.

Payments in the cloud (2009)

Many of you may wonder what the hell cloud computing all that is about. Well, cloud is the big buzz in the tech sector because it's new, glitzy, sexy and brings together all the stuff that's gone before. From the old days of bureaux and mainframes, through outsourcing, SaaS and ASPs, cloud does it all.

So what is cloud computing? The simplest definition is hosted services using the internet, but it covers a lot more than that including delivery of software, hardware and infrastructure as a pay-as-you-go service. You just pay for what you use.

There are lots of discussions about this right now, as Google and Amazon have made cloud computing a key offer in their portfolio of services.

Equally, to illustrate the power of cloud one of the best examples is Animoto. Animoto is a small website that went from hardly any users to millions over a weekend, thanks to the viral effect of Facebook, and they managed to handle the sudden upsurge in demand by just paying for compute power provided by Amazon. It's not just about scalability, however.

I thought I would share a story of one area where I see this taking off big time.

Payments processing. You heard me: payments processing. Cloud computing is perfect for payments processing.

Here are three examples.

SEPA is here but, for one of my bank buddies, SEPA Direct Debits and the PSD is a pain in the backside. You see, they don't have any customers who want or need cross-border direct debits. Not a single one. So they've decided to handle SEPA Direct Debits (SDD) on an exceptions basis, with the view they might need to process three or four a year.

If it spikes above that, however, which they don't believe it will ,but you never know, then they would like a SDD cloud computing service to handle that. A secure SDD cloud service, of course, which could be delivered easily by the EBA or one of the commercial clearing companies.

Which brings me to the second example.

Now that SDD is here, by November 2010 every single bank in Europe must be reachable through the SDD scheme. That's the law under Regulation 2560, so like it or lump it, you gotta be able to receive those debits in an SDD format. In other words, you should be able to send a direct debit payment in the SDD scheme to any bank account holder in the 27 countries of Europe, and the bank should be able to receive that instruction and process it.

So we all start thinking of standards and bringing in new systems that use XML and ISO20022 ... except we don't have to do that.

Howsabout a cloud conversion service to take anything you have winging its way over to your systems and they convert it to your systems formats as it's flying over. A conversion service which can handle the odd message or the many on an as needed pay-as-you-go basis. Lovely.

Which brings me to the third example.

Banks are looking at how to create added value in this post-SEPA commoditised payments world by talking about corporate services and value-add through real-time information provision, e-invoicing, financial supply chain management and more.

So howsabout a bank created financial supply chain solution through the cloud? The corporate customer just has to plug their back office ERP systems, general ledger, invoicing, account receivables and payables, and the cloud will just automatically keep all their fields of financial information updated and managed in a real-time service.

Financial clouds will start to take off over the next five years. The only challenge will be where the legal liability lies when your cloud goes down, as happened when Microsoft's cloud services for T-Mobile exploded, losing all the customer data for T-Mobile's Sidekick users.

This may seem inconsequential, but the new Sidekick has been heavily marketed as a lifestyle phone with camera, 3G access, email and more, and the cloud was the place to keep all of your contacts, photos, updates, social messaging, etc. In other words, the failure of the cloud, in this case, lost everyone's digital lives.

That's pretty consequential (had Microsoft heard of disaster recovery, business continuity, etc?).

Who's accountable is half the question but the other half is how much damage such explosions can cause to your credibility rather than the cloud provider's?

So yes, there are still questions about cloud but these will get fixed. In the meantime, if you're not ready for cloud then you better get ready, as there is no way that a bank can continue to buy servers and systems that are only used on a Friday peak volume the day before Christmas.

No way.

And that's one of the big points about cloud computing: getting the technology to move from being a high capital expenditure and investment to just being a variable operational expense on the basis of usage.

6

If that last point doesn't ram it home, then perhaps this point will.

One bank said to me during this research that the typical cycle time compute power they use would have an internal cross-charge from the IT Division of U$200 for every $1 of cost for the same compute power from Amazon EC2.

For a general analytic process, he was being charged $12,000 or more per night by the internal IT division for what would cost $60 from Amazon.

That's why cloud computing will take off in financial services.

Innovation in payments (Part 1) (2009)

I was asked to write about innovation in payments last week, and so here's the first of three parts. The first part will focus upon retail payments innovation; the second, corporate payments; and the third, trade settlement.

First, what is innovation? My definition is short and sweet:

"Innovation: the method of creating compelling new ways of doing things that open up new markets or radically disrupt existing markets."

Innovation does not have to be positive, increase value etc, as innovation could just as easily destroy things and eradicate value. The internet has destroyed the value of newspapers and television. It's turned news and views into free access for all, as well as connecting individuals to individuals. It is not positive for the incumbents and may be positive for the customer, although some may say not. For example, how many of us would see the destruction of the BBC, CNN and NBC as being good? Can the blogosphere and YouTuber replace the value of good news reporting and media production?

These are questions we have yet to answer, so I'm on the fence a little about whether innovation has to be positive and create value.

What innovation really needs to do is to show something compelling. Compelling means that people use it. The reason YouTube works is that I can send my stuff there and share it. The blogosphere has created news reporting in real-time from a potential 3.5 billion news reporters. The access to news is more global and comprehensive than it has ever been ... but is the news believable?

The fact that Wikipedia has a small amount of misreporting is not a good thing is it? And when websites report celebrities as being dead when it's blatantly untrue, you sit in a mass of confusion rather than truth.

Anyways, that's a precursor to a debate about defining innovation and the value of the new web worlds, rather than innovation in payments. Nevertheless, it is important to get the definition right, so I come back to my definition of innovation as being a method of creating compelling new ways of doing things that open up new markets or radically disrupt existing markets, before discussing payments innovations.

So what compelling new payments markets are being created or disrupted in the retail payments world?

Certainly, mobile payments and prepaid are innovating retail payments. They are opening up new markets for electronic services that displace cash. That is why they are good for the producers, the banks, as any cash displacement makes finance more efficient because it's getting rid of paper. And paper accounts for six out of seven transactions today.

But mobile and prepaid have been trying to disrupt this space for half a decade. I first started talking about mobile as a payments mechanism back in 2004 when NTT DoCoMo started showing us the way.

Therefore, the fact that mobile is now mainstream is no longer innovative. The innovation has happened. A bit like online payments with PayPal happened. And prepaid is an innovation – creating new compelling markets based upon existing technologies – but it's also happened.

These things are here. That's why I don't call them innovations, as innovation is what I look for before it happens. When you see Web 2.0, it's too late. When you see Facebook and wonder whether to compete with it, it's too late. It's already dominating. When you see everyone talking about mobile payments, it's too late. They've taken off. When you hear everyone discussing prepaid cards, it's too late. Everyone's got one.

The fact is that most banks are fast followers, so they do wait until it's too late. Then they launch their mobile and prepaid services. And they succeed. They succeed because a bank never finds it too late due to the protection of their markets from new entrants and the inertia of their customers to change provider. That does not mean that banks should not innovate, however.

So what is innovative today?

Wireless payments. This is contactless, but it's more than that. It's wireless, free-form payments built into objects, clothing, watches ... anything. Wirelessly communicating electronic payment tools for consumers. That's innovative.

Wireless communication works by placing the receiver and emitter in near-field communication. The receiver or emitter can be in any form of device. A phone, a card, or a watch or earring. Anything that can take an RFID chip (today) or some form of wireless chip (tomorrow). The chips are really small, minute, tiny. So tiny that you won't be able to see them with the human eye in some instances.

As a result, the chips can be woven into cloth, placed in a tooth filling or embedded in bricks and tarmac.

Money for Nothing and your Cheques for Free

Everything communicates. Everything knows where everything else is. So we think that's scary? Well, who thought the internet was scary when it started to take off? Who rebutted mobile telephony as pure yuppiedom?

Things take off faster than you think and, by the time you see them, they are mainstream and it's too late.

So, the near future is wireless communications enabling wireless payments ... and a lot more. And it will all be based upon geo-location and proximity. Knowing that you are walking past the shoe shop, you get an advert for your favourite Geo shoes. Knowing that you are near the O2 stadium, you get a promotion for tonight's concert as tickets are still available (must be a rubbish act). And knowing that you need to sort out your overdraft, you get a request to visit with the bank manager as you near the branch (oh no!).

All of this is likely in the very near term.

How near? Well, in hong Kong recently, my cab was equipped with 'GPS Based Advertising'. As the cab drives around Hong Kong, you get adverts tailored to the vicinity you are in. Come and shop at Harbour City! Visit Honeychurch Antiques in Central now! Dive into the Computer Centre in Mongkok for very good deals! As the taxi moves, everything changes ... advert by advert.

Now imagine this in the payments context. You see the ad for Armani and wave at the screen ... the suit is in the post. You walk past a billboard for Geo and bish, bash, bosh ... the shoes arrive tomorrow. You get the promo for tonight's concert at the O2 and ding! the RFID code for your ticket entry is delivered to your phone.

This is not the future. It is right here, right now.

And that's what I call innovation, along with a few other things that will come into the blog in the next two weeks.

Innovation in payments (Part 2) (2009)

In this second part, I thought I would take a closer look at what is innovatory in the corporate world of payments.

Many of us would immediately start talking about e-invoicing, supply chains and working capital. Sure, there is some innovation in those areas but the picture is bigger than this.

First, a little clarity of definitions, as per my lingo.

Commercial payments are the domain of the large transaction banks and their multinational and global clients. These are the mega corporations of the world we refer to affectionately as corporates. It is not exclusively owned by these banks, as there are many national companies with domestic banks providing commercial banking very nicely thank you ... it's just that my mind wanders off into global processors with global clients when I think about commercial payments.

This is because there is a big change taking place here. Until recently, these corporates had been fairly undemanding of their banks. They were happy to have the odd lunch with their banker, who would fine dine and ego-boost them for an hour or two every month.

Taking their treasury operations, charging solid fees for transactions and generally making a good mint out of cross-border payments was food and drink to the banker. This is where the money was to be made without stretching too far or too hard. In particular, get the corporate to do their dealings through the bank via a proprietary link and you had 'em for life.

After all, once the corporates general ledgers were hard-wired to the bank's systems, it was all but suicide for the corporate engine to switch to anyone else. This was especially true as the savings made just would not be worth the effort involved. A few cents here and a few pence there, per transaction, goes hardly noticed in the global wheels of commerce.

That was until standards arrived.

Standards. The bug-bear of some, the bane of many and the blessing for the few – the few who can work out how to leverage scale and exploit standards for volume savings. This is what SWIFT does well – exploits standards for volume savings – but, until recently, SWIFT's volume savings were purely gifted to the banking community. The corporate was still waiting for the benefit. This is the struggle that has been taking place within the SWIFT community for the past decade and, to a lesser extent, still rages today. How do you give savings to the corporate and how do you allow corporates to exploit standards, when all it does is erode margins for their current payments provider and allows the corporate to become a rate tart with easy switching to any other bank.

Tough.

The days of proprietary lock-ins are over. SWIFT has recognised this and is ever more embracing of the corporate community for this reason. Forget payments, transaction and messaging ... SWIFT's future is all around secure information exchange between banks, between businesses and, you never know, but one day in the future, maybe even between individuals.

And banks are now scrabbling harder and harder to keep their corporate clients happy and well served for this reason. Some of us would say, "Isn't that how it's supposed to be? Shouldn't banks always serve their customer well?" ... yeah, but it hasn't been that way in the past because once you got the sucker, they couldn't get away. But now they can and so let's look at what the banks are doing to serve their corporate clients better.

This was a question posed by Gary Wright, Director for International Payments with Royal Bank of Scotland last week at the Financial Services Club.

The evening focused upon the opportunities and issues with real-time payments and this is the innovation in corporate banking and payments that is taking place today, as we speak.

Real time.

Real-time money movements intra-corporate and inter-corporate, intra-bank and inter-bank. Real-time payments across borders and continents. Real-time trade flows of information and risk. That's where the corporate money is at.

For a bank, you see, the old world of reporting as the bank wanted, when the bank wanted, how the bank wanted and what the bank wanted to report, was how it worked. There was no incentive to leverage the information flows the bank had access to, which was a privilege. Banks have access to masses of trade data, but where was the incentive to tap into that data? For many, with customers locked in via proprietary network connections that were hard-wired into back office systems, the incentive just was not there.

But today, with open networking via cloud-based systems that plug and play into SAP and ORACLE Enterprise Resource Planning suites of software, there is a huge incentive for a bank to re-engineer itself back into the corporate value chain. And that's exactly what banks are starting to deliver.

The question is, what is it exactly that corporates want?

Gary answered this with a great slide. Just one slide, but a real goodie.

Here it is:

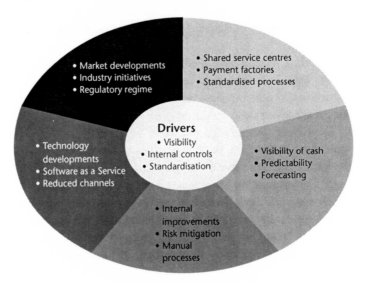

- Market developments
- Industry initiatives
- Regulatory regime

- Shared service centres
- Payment factories
- Standardised processes

Drivers
- Visibility
- Internal controls
- Standardisation

- Technology developments
- Software as a Service
- Reduced channels

- Visibility of cash
- Predictability
- Forecasting

- Internal improvements
- Risk mitigation
- Manual processes

What this slide shows is the range of drivers that corporates have towards real-time services and improved delivery of services from the payments provider. The fact is that working capital is the issue. Without good visibility and transparency of working capital, corporates are stymied into a vacuum of ignorance.

It reminded me of a debate I had about four years ago where we talked about cash pooling and netting. One software firm had created a system that provided a real-time view of every corporate client of the bank's cash positions globally. With the click of button, the bank's risk managers could see which clients were exposed where and when, and manage the situation.

The problem the software vendor had was that no bank wanted their system. Why would a bank spend millions on a system that told them their clients were possibly exposed in real-time? Intraday or end-of-day would do. That's why the system wasn't selling.

14

But guess what? Turn that on its head and start talking about real-time cash management for corporate treasury today as an information service and guess what? You've got a winner. The corporate treasurer mindful of his global financial positioning loves the idea of real-time. And this is what banks are now buying into as a value-add service that differentiates them from the pack.

The more real-time service, the more real-time information, the more real-time movement to decrease fraud and risks, the more real-time capability to see how to improve ROI and decrease losses, the more a corporate client will love ya'.

And that's what banks want. Not to be loved ... but to keep their corporate client.

Anyways, the net:net on innovations in transaction services for commercial banking is that if you aren't enriching your clients with real-time information services about their use of your bank's services, then you're missing a trick because the competition is doing just that.

And by the way, e-invoicing and related innovations in supply chain management play right into that space too.

Payment innovation (Part 3) (2009)

In the securities settlement markets, we've spent years trying to break down barriers to clearing and settlement ... and most of those barriers are still there. We wonder what to do about it, and regulation seems the only answer.

Or is it?

As we look at innovations in payments this week is the final thoughts on this as we study payments in the trading room and investment markets.

There are clearly some things afoot which will change things. The first is that everything is real-time or supra real-time. Sure, we talk about fast and scalable systems, but in the trading arena we're talking not just fast but super-fast.

What's super-fast? Well, a human blink of an eye takes about 200 milliseconds or a fifth of one second. Today's trading systems trade in under 200 microseconds. There are 1,000 microseconds in a millisecond, so we can trade 1,000 times faster than the blink of an eye. That's super-fast.

This is the world of latency, which really does bring in a new focus on real-time. For example, I spent last week at a fascinating open day for Deutsche Bourse's IT , at which a chart was presented by Colt Telecom that shows linkages between London, Frankfurt and Chicago, with latency of 50 milliseconds or thereabouts. In other words, four messages can move between Frankfurt and Chicago in the time it took you to blink. Another chart showed how all the exchanges are linked via high speed dark fibre 1 gigabit per second (1G) and up to 10G. The view is that, by 2011, these lines will be moving data at 6.4 terabits per second (t/s)! This means we will be moving from a world where it takes about 0.5 seconds to send a message right around the world once (two blinks), to one where that global transaction of data could move around the world in a complete cycle in under one millisecond (blink and you miss it).

This is the real-time world. Now think about liquidity, risk, clearing and settlement and imagine a world where, as you trade:

◆ Your complete picture of liquidity positions are transparent to all traders internally;

◆ Your liquidity risk exposures, market and credit risk exposures and more are visible to all counterparties in real-time;

◆ Your trade reporting and pricing is visible to all regulatory and supervisory authorities in real-time;

- And real-time clearing takes place as part of trade execution.

This world is not a future vision, but a reality. Eurex, for example, thanks to being tightly coupled with a clearing system (Eurex Clearing), are already offering real-time clearing.

Meanwhile, we have regulators moving further and further towards information reporting duties that go far beyond today's methods. That is why real-time trade and risk reporting will be a reality in the near-term. End of day just doesn't cut it. Intra-day doesn't manage it. Real-time everything. That's the future of investment markets. Real-time visibility and transparency for all counterparties to manage risk.

Mmmm ... now it gets interesting.

A real-time global pulse (2009)

As we use low latency systems, faster payments, Twitter and other technologies, we silently watch the revolution of our world from local to global communities, and to a real-time global pulse.

The thing is, do you ever stop to notice? The fact that you can trade in a millionth of a millionth of a second, transfer monies at light speed, and share news from Beijing to Birmingham as it happens, is the world we live in today.

You can find out what is happening in the economy, business, banking and life faster than the major TV news channels. Equally, as news is reported, you can supplant the news with feet on the street views by tapping into this global pulse.

This was brought home to me as I watched the April 1st G20 protests in Twitter, YouTube and live on the BBC News24 and Sky News*. The mind-meld of real-time social media channels with news media channels created a world of almost like being there, even though you weren't. Like being omniscient, even though you aren't.

This global real-time pulse is now as true for the world of finance as it is for the world of news. We can operate a global brain pulse of knowledge about stocks and trading and investments. We can provide real-time dashboards for cash management and pooling across corporate supply chains as an information service. We can run a real-time money transfer service between migrants in America and their remote families in Asia. We can even create a real-time pulse check for fraud and money laundering. That's partly what the changes to cover payments is meant to achieve.

However, in financial services generally, this is happening and we are getting there ...

... but it is happening very, v e r y, v e r y s l o w l y.

What's the issue? If we can trade and socialise in real-time, why can't we buy and sell in real-time? Is it down to the very nature of fraud and all the legal meanderings that go around such commercial trading activities? The fact is that if you pay in real-time and, later, want to revoke the payment, who is liable? You pay in real-time and fraud occurs, who is at fault?

One view would be that, like cash, you should be able to make payments in real-time. This would make a transaction irrevocable. You do the deal and it's done. This approach would revolutionise finance, as there would be no issues over trading any size of goods. Once the money is transacted in real-time, it's yours.

That was meant to be the point of the UK's Faster Payments, but it hasn't happened.

On the one hand, Faster Payments is only for standing orders, telephone and internet payments, where the security measures mean that most of the payments would need a personal authorisation to take place. Therefore, if the payment was incorrect after the fact then ... tough. It's your fault. That's why card payments aren't included, as they are far too open to abusive practices today.

On the other hand, you could take the view that a real-time payment doesn't necessarily mean what it says on tin. It's only trading bits and bytes of data you see, not real cash. No real money is actually moved between the accounts. Therefore, you could say that the electronic transaction takes place in real-time, but monetary movements are not signed and sealed until end-of-day.

Just transfer the bits and bytes of real-time data files between accounting systems and follow up with real-time monetary movements later.

Oh yes, that's what we do anyway isn't it? Transact the data and then, later, settle the money. So, real-time payments should be OK, shouldn't they? It's only trading data after all.

And meanwhile, if you're worried about the fraud of real-time payments then real-time fraud detection should overcome this. For example, if you suspect it's a fraudulent transaction then, in real-time, a random security question can be generated at the POS or online.

Then who needs PINs and one-time passwords?

In real-time, if you want to spend £10,000 on a car on eBay ... no worries. Just tell us, in real-time, what's your post code, name one direct debit on your account and tell us your first pet's name? If you can't answer those, then choose from a list.

So here's a near-term vision for real-time payments.

At payment time, whether online or offline, internet, telephone or POS, you no longer enter a PIN or password. You just to answer a random question from a list such as:

Enter the number that represents the last payment from your account;

Enter the data (DDMMYY) of the last ATM transaction you made;

Enter an amount that leaves your account by direct debit each month;

Enter your postcode/zipcode;

Enter your main telephone number as registered on your account;

Enter your main personal code (could be a PIN or passport number, birth date - your choice)

... etc.

Money for Nothing and your Cheques for Free

Note, this list would change every time you pay and would probably only apply for payments over let's say 100 units of £, € or $.

Real-time everything, including real-time payments with real-time security.

Now we're cooking.

* Just noticed I naturally phrased this line with the term "watched in" social media and "watched on" traditional media. This shows how you are far more engaged "in" an interactive world of media, rather than the one-way receiving "on" traditional media.

Fragmented payments in a connected world (2008)

If payments is just transferring a file electronically between a sender and a recipient these days, why is it so darned complicated?

Bearing in mind, the internet connects everyone and everything electronically, how come we have so many disparate payments infrastructures? From retail to wholesale payments, clearing and settlement, we do have a bit of a worldwide mesh. The DTCC, Chips, Fedwire, Vocalink, Equens, STEP2, TARGET2, Euroclear, Clearstream, LCH.Clearnet, BOJ-NET, CLS, Master-Card, Visa ... now I know I'm mixing up a lot of stuff in that line but it's far from exhaustive.

There are literally hundreds of processors involved in our payments processes but surely we should be moving towards a single, standardised pipe around the world for payments, clearing and settlement? That's what we have today as a baseline platform for technology, the internet, so why not for payments?

There are few examples of global processors today. I guess the ones that immediately come to mind would be CLS, SWIFT, Visa, MasterCard and PayPal. Most banks, citizens and corporates can pretty much hook up to one of those somewhere around the world and make a payment to the other side of the world. But why is the rest of our payments processing, clearing and settlement structures so fragmented?

I guess because they all grew up as regionally or domestically isolated payments and clearing hubs that suited the regional or domestic operation. Equally, many relate to the complexity of the payment operation, whether it is high or low value, whether it involves company and fiscal laws related to cross-border operations and related matters.

But all of that is changing. We are moving away from isolated operations to integrated operations. Again, this has been driven by the internet. The internet has transformed our world, so that everything is connected today. That was the point of yesterday's discussion of general banking, where customers are now connected from Manchester to Mumbai, Vermont to Vietnam, Shanghai to San Francisco and Brussels to Brazil. There are no disconnections electronically in today's society. That's why most folks cannot understand why sending a payment anywhere on the planet is a problem.

Take PayPal. PayPal's not even 10 years old, but it allows 164 million accounts to pay for things in 190 countries and 17 currencies to the tune of around $5 billion a month. Now that's a global service for consumers. Yes, it sits on top of the entire gunk underneath but it hides it. That's why PayPal is successful. PayPal, to Joe Public, appears to be a single, global retail brand for payments online.

That's what we need for high value payments, clearing and settlement. A PayPal-style brand that hides all the complexity behind it, allowing corporates, custodians, banks and exchanges to all plug-and-play worldwide without having to worry about what lies beneath.

Money for Nothing and your Cheques for Free

That's what MasterCard and Visa provide corporates: global brands for retail payments, without worrying about all the banks that process behind them. That's what SWIFT provides banks: a global brand for financial transactions, without worrying about all of the banks that process behind them.

But let's look out longer-term and think about where we really want to go and come back to Europe's Single Euro Payments Area (SEPA) and the Payment Services Directive (PSD), as an example of the trend.

SEPA, the PSD and the whole agenda of Europe is driven by a recognition that we cannot exist with fragmented payments processing across Europe. That is not competitive and having 27 countries with 27 ACHs, 27 clearing operations, 27 real-time gross settlement systems and so on and so forth, just does not make sense. So we're consolidating and collapsing the whole lot down to one ... or two ... or three or four or more.

Regardless, we will end up with far less payments technologies across Europe as a result of SEPA and the PSD. Maybe not one ACH and one clearing system, but far less than 27 or more.

But that is still not going to be good enough, is it? We have one internet. We don't have several, although there may be several versions. We have one mobile network. We don't have several, although there are several variations. We have one standard for shipping worldwide. It's called a container, and has standard sizes recognised by every port across the world. That's why we can ship goods cheaply worldwide.

In each of the above examples, there may be regional variations, but the standards overcome the variations.

The internet has great complexity underneath, but the bases of IPv4, IPv6, WiMAX, Bluetooth and more make it easy to connect. As a result, we can access the internet worldwide, with any laptop or wireless device.

Mobile telecommunications is horrendously complex, but GSM, GPRS, 3G and more make it easy to connect. That is why we can travel and make calls worldwide with confidence, using Triband handsets.

Every country receives different sizes of container but the fact that ISO has limited the size to just five: 20 feet (6.1 metres), 40 feet (12.2 metres), 45 feet (13.7 metres), 48 feet (14.6 metres), and 53 feet (16.2 metres) containers means that we can ship worldwide, with confidence that the container can be received at the other end and unloaded.

That is the future world of payments.

There will be single platforms that are global brands that standardise our world of payments and hide the regional variants that lie beneath. We will get to a global clearing, global settlement, global messaging, global bank and account identification standard. ISO, SWIFT, the banking community and collaboration will get us there so that, eventually, we will have single standards to automate every part of the payments, clearing and settlement process.

At that point, we will have integrated payments in a connected world.

I just wonder how long we'll take to get there?

Payments: the next generation (2006)

(The following is an extract from a longer report written by Chris Skinner.)

It's payments, Jim, but not as we know it ... These are the voyages of the Payments Enterprise. Our electronic mission: to boldly pay where no-one has paid before.

We live in a world where we can communicate with anyone, anywhere for less than the cost of a packet of chewing gum. We can teleport ourselves around the world from the comfort of our home virtually through Google Earth, and we can send messages anywhere instantaneously through emails and texts. We can physically travel around the world for less than the cost of a train journey, and we can buy goods from the other side of the world and receive them within 24 hours.

We are living in the 21st century. We are also living through the greatest commercial revolution in history. The revolution of the networked world. This revolution began when *Star Trek* first launched four decades ago and now, the *Star Trek* age has arrived. So why are we still paying for goods and services with ancient forms of payments, such as cash, cheques and cards, and what will happen when this *Star Trek* world finally hits the payments markets?

Major headlines from this report

◆ Payment innovations occur each time there is a revolution in commerce;

◆ The last three commercial revolutions created coins, cheques and cards; what will the latest revolution create?

◆ Many believe that contactless, mobile and biometric micropayments are the answer, replacing previous forms of payment such as cards and cash;

◆ This report demonstrates that such thinking is completely wrong: future payments will not be contactless, mobile or biometric; there is another form of payment for the future. (....)

Three historical revolutions created three forms of payments:

◆ The agricultural revolution created coins;

◆ The industrial revolutions was fuelled by the growth of banknotes and bank cheques; and

◆ The service revolution required the use of debit and credit cards

In the 21st century, we are experiencing another revolution. An electronic revolution.

What form of payment will this revolution create? ... I think of it as being about the networked world. The networked world is wired and electric. The networked world communicates and is connected 24*7. The networked world allows goods and services, thoughts and ideas, sex and pornography, travel and commerce, music and entertainment – life – to travel around the world freely and easily.

Borderless capital and liquidity. Borderless commerce. Borderless banking.

OK, we are not quite there yet. We still have friction and issues between countries and nations. We still have tariffs and protectionism. But we are moving rapidly away from the ability of governments to stop such activity. After all, just think of how challenged governments are by taxation of goods on the internet. How the Chinese are challenged to maintain censorship on the internet. How the music and film industry have struggled to maintain control over copyright.

And so, to payments.

Payments in a networked world

Payments are being forced to adapt to the networked world, in the same way that governments are being forced to adapt. However, the adaptation is not the obvious one that you may think we would identify.

For example, after three revolutions in history which created cash, cheques and cards, what do you think the network revolution will create?

Micropayments?

Contactless payments?

Money for Nothing and your Cheques for Free

Mobile payments?
Wearable payments?
Biometric payments?

Let's look at each of these in turn.

Micropayments

Although micropayments means sub-$1 payments to some, as in cent or even micro-cent payments, in this area micropayments today alludes more to payments that could not be processed profitably by banks electronically using previous means, as in sub-$5 payments. Micropayments of sub-$5 account for about $40 billion of all payments worldwide today, according to Jupiter Media.

How come? Because micropayments have been driven by the demands for online and mobile services.

In the former case, we can all point to the success of PayPal who now have more customers than Bank of America, Wells Fargo, Barclays Bank and Deutsche Bank combined, and more credit-card accepting merchants PayPal-enabled than the combined number of merchants for Visa and MasterCard.

Transacting over $1,000 a second, PayPal is the gorilla of online payments and part of its success is not just being owned by eBay, but having a unique model of business that supports micropayments. Think about it. Before PayPal, how many sub-$5 payments would you have transacted. Today, it is easy.

In the words of one of PayPal's founders, Elon Musk:

"A vital competitive advantage was that PayPal had significantly lower transaction fees ... part of the secret behind PayPal's much lower fee structure was having a low cost way to authenticate a customer's bank account, so that we could pull money into our system for a few cents per transaction."

In other words, because it cost PayPal peanuts to transact, it cots the customer peanuts to transact and so the customer could transact in peanut amounts. Not in peanuts though, but in real dollars, Euros and yen.

Is it any wonder that PayPal's transaction volumes continue to break all records, with $37.75 billion transacted in 2006, a 37% increase over 2005 ($27.51 billion) which was a 45% increase over 2004 ($18.5 billion). But not all of that is micropayments. In fact, much of that is macropayments. In fact, micropayments in PayPal account for less than 5% of sales. Even so, that is $2 billion per annum.

Is it any wonder that Booz Allen Hamilton forecast a number of critical impacts that micropayments would have on card issuers and acquirers. In a 2006 study, they found that existing debit and credit card firms could lose up to 30% of transactions to online retailers offering PayPal and Google Checkout.

Having said that, if PayPal only accounts for $2 billion of micropayments, where are the other $38 billion coming from? A great deal is coming from music downloads. For example, iTunes generated $634 million in Apple's Q1 2007 revenues compared to $491 million for the same quarter the year before. The digital media research firm comScore Networks reckon that Apple's iTunes Store sales rose 84% in the first three quarters of 2006 versus the same period in 2005, with a 67% increase in customers. The report also found that the number of people visiting the iTunes Store increased significantly from 11.2 million unique visitors in November 2005 rising 85% to 20.8 million unique visitors in November 2006.

So what? Well, each tune is priced at $0.99. That is a micropayment.

Equally, look at ringtones and games which sell on mobile telephones today. Ringtones alone are already outselling traditional CD sales for music, with each download costing under $5. In 2006, ringtone sales were estimated to be worth $5 billion with

Money for Nothing and your Cheques for Free

the best-selling Crazy Frog from Jamba generating almost $500 million in sales on its own. Those are micropayments.

Between online payments, PayPal payments, downloads of tunes and articles, games and ringtones, the micropayments market is burgeoning. But most of that is driven by traditional payments using credit cards. So, it's not the revolution in payments we are looking for in the networked world. It is, instead, purely a logical extension of electronic payments being taken into smaller and smaller amounts through the increasingly affordable technologies available today.

What about contactless payments then – are they the information revolution's payments product?

Contactless payments

Contactless payments are based upon RFID or NFC chips being integrated into a plastic card. RFID, Radio Frequency Identification, chips require close proximity whereas NFC, Near Field Communication, chips transmit wirelessly and can be received over longer distance. The former is being used for most contactless payments programmes, such as American Express's Express-Pay. MasterCard's PayPass, and Visa Contactless. The latter is just starting to be picked up by for use in mobile telephones and for access to stadiums and theatres to replace ticketing, and is targeted for use in mobile phones.

This payment method is pretty standard already, even though a number of countries are yet to roll-out programmes that support contactless payments, and is proving to be a low-cost, robust and proven technology.

The actual coverage of the markets for contactless is also huge as, for example, Datamonitor estimated the total value of all cash payments under $25 in the USA were worth over $724 billion in 2004. That's a lot of cash to get rid of and both micropayments and contactless payments will erode the traditional cash market areas.

In particular, stores and customers like contactless 'tap and go' payments. In a study by MasterCard in 2006, their contactless system PayPass was being used by about 10 million consumers in 32,000 merchant locations with the following results:

◆ 36% increase in usage per account;

◆ 45% increase in total transactions per account;

◆ The average transaction, credit or debit, is approximately US$20;

◆ Consumers use their payment cards 18% more often on average;

◆ 75% of all PayPass transactions are for purchases below $25; and

◆ 45% of all transactions are for purchases below $10.

Why is this happening? Because the consumer is no longer limited by that amount of cash in their pocket and, according to another study by Javelin Research, 84% of users thought it was as safe as or even safer than credit cards.

This is why various organisations forecast contactless payments will transact around $40 billion a year. But contactless still requires a card today, so it does not displace a prior revolution's creation. Equally, contactless is bounded by being quick which means no authentication, so they are no use as a means to make higher value transactions. In other words, contactless payments are not the end game of the networked world revolution.

What about mobile payments then?

Mobile payments

Mobile, to be honest, is just an extension of contactless with two major forms of mobile payments in operation: the text-based messaging payment and the contactless chip-based payment.

The former is the service that has been used for a while now based upon SMS text messaging a number with the amount, for example, when you travel through London and need to pay the 'Congestion Charge' – an £8 ($16) tax for driving in London – you can pay by SMS text message. This is also the approach being used by PayPal Mobile, where you text 63336 to any firm displaying the PayPal Mobile logo and the payment is taken there and then from you PayPal account and the goods are yours.

However, text messaging a chunky, clunky way of paying when compared to the contactless chip phone, such as NTT DoCoMo's Felica phone. The Felica phone was the first contactless mobile telephone payment service in the world, and was launched in Japan in 2005.

The way it works is that you hold the phone over the payments station, a terminal not dissimilar to the contactless payments terminals used above, and the payment is made from, in the Felica case, a mobile wallet called Edy that is associated with the mobile telephone account.

The latter approach is therefore one that is simple, fast, easy and convenient, combining the best of both contactless and mobile payments. As a result, it is increasingly likely to be the mainstream form of contactless payment over time. Why? Because Nokia have a deal with MasterCard PayPass to integrate this capability into their future phones, and have already rolled this out in trial from with Citibank in New York and are likely to do the same across many other U.S. and European cities during 2007.

Having said that, if you can put a chip into a telephone why stop there? Why not put a chip into a watch, ring, cuff link or even stitch the chip into the cloth of a jacket, blouse or shirt?

That may sound silly, but that is exactly what some banks and providers are doing. For example, Chinatrust Bank launched a special Swatch-style watch during the summer of 2006 to celebrate the Football World Cup in Germany. Again, MasterCard PayPass was selected as the payment mechanism, and this delivered a contactless wearable payments device. This example, along with several others such as the JCB Watch in Japan, demonstrate that there is no reason why a bank should not take offer their customers designer goods to promote there accounts, and even take this further by designing such gifts in other jewellery or clothing. Give it a few years, and I'll buy my suit from the bank ...

The only downside is that it is still all based upon RFID and NFC chips, and therefore has the same restrictions as contactless payments, such that mobile and wearable payments are only good for low value transactions requiring no authentication.

However, combine contactless, mobile and wearable payments with biometrics and surely that solves the issue?

No.

Biometric payments

Biometrics is an area that is taking off rapidly as a secure authentication mechanism for managing national borders. Passports and identification cards incorporating fingerprint, palm-print, voice, signature, iris, retina or other body parts as a form of identification and authentication is becoming the government mantra in these days of terrorism and concerns over national security. These technologies are all growing in terms of scalability, resilience, usage and stature and yes, they all enable secure and reliable authentication.

Many of us still have concerns around security of the individual if biometrics are used for recognition and authentication, as in the removal of hands and eyeballs is a potential liability, but many are experimenting with the idea of combining such recognition technologies with a payments method.

In particular, biometric identification is proving to be successful with those individuals who would have traditionally struggled with identification or authentication, such as those who do not have passports or driving licences, or those who are illiterate. This is the reason why Banco Azteca in Mexico has one of the largest biometric payments card rollouts of any bank in the world, with over 8 million customers making 200,000 biometric payments daily using their fingerprints. Similar programs are in use with Bank Danamon in Indonesia and ICICI Bank in India to reach the rural farmer who is illiterate and therefore cannot sign their name.

Although some of us therefore may feel that the biometric payment concept is uncomfortable, because it is intrusive to the individual, many are supportive of more widespread usage. For example, you even find biometrics in use at Universal Studios and Disney theme parks in Florida these days to secure lockers using fingerprints whilst most airports now offer fast track immigration using iris recognition for regular travellers. Equally, most passports are moving towards biometrics, with fingerprints and iris scans as part of the identification. Further examples include US immigration, where fingerprints are part of the identification checks as you enter any US border controls.

As governments and theme parks move towards increasing usage of biometrics, so citizens will expect this service to be used. Therefore, it will become acceptable for banks to leverage these capabilities to improve services through convenience.

In fact, it is particularly interesting to note that most biometric trials with consumers so far have been through retailers, who see the deployment of biometrics as increasing transaction size and improving speed of checkout.

For example, a recent report by Sanford Bernstein found that the use of biometrics for retailing reduced the potential for fraud and identity theft, speeded up the checkout process, and most importantly, lowered transaction processing fees for retailers, improving their bottom line. A 20% reduction in processing costs at big-box discounters like Wal-Mart over the next several years could result in a 3% to 4% increase in earnings per share by 2009, the report estimated.

In another trial by US grocery chain Piggly Wiggly using a technology called Pay-By-Touch, the retailer discovered that biometric payments were 70% faster than traditional forms of payment.

Finally, a 2003 Federal Trade Commission survey found 13% of the 10 million cases of identity theft occurred during a retail payment transaction and so increasing security through biometrics is seen as the retail solution.

That is why it is likely that banks will ignore the rollout of biometric payments at their peril as retailers see this as a critical program. I think it is especially interesting, for example, that the largest bank-based biometric program from Banco Azteca may be also due, in part, to the fact that the bank is owned by Grupo Electra, a major Mexican retail group.

So, you are probably now thinking that the combination of contactless, mobile and wearable payments with biometrics is my answer to the payments revolution that evolves out of our networked world revolution. That this will be the solution that will be on a par with the creation of cash, cheques and cards – the payments solutions from the last three revolutionary periods of commerce.

Nope. Almost, but not quite.

The fact is that all of these forms of payment are mere offshoots of the longer-term. Just as the typewriter gave way to the word processor gave way to the PC gave way to the laptop gave way to the telephone gave way to the blackberry and so on, the information revolution is an ongoing march of change, not some stultifying moment in time. Just as WAP-banking, SMS-banking, text-banking, email-banking and back to WAP-banking has evolved, so will payments.

Therefore, today's micro, mobile, contactless, biometric payments will eventually evolve into a true form of new world payments. What will be the final form?

Payments: the Next Generation

We cannot be sure, but here is my contention.

The final form of payments will be based upon an implanted chip and will be invisible payments. All of today's payments are chip-based and the chip is getting more powerful and more capable. Just as today's laptop is the equivalent of yesterday's mainframe computer, today's mobile telephone is the equivalent of yesterday's laptop and today's silicon chip is the equivalent of yesterday's smartphone. Moore's law of twice as much processing power for half the cost continues to apply, as much to chips as to computers.

Think about Mondex for example. The Smart Card of 1996 was expensive and unusable – the EMV card of today is cheap and easy. The RFID and NFC chip of today is cheap and basic; the wireless chip of tomorrow will be cheap and powerful. Probably as powerful as today's most capable computers and laptops.If that is the case, what would you do with it?

My guess is that you would be using chips to automate almost everything from washing and cooking to mowing the lawn to driving cars. We are almost there already. Today, I can buy a BMW that can monitor its speed on cruise control, and slow down or speed up automatically based upon surrounding traffic speeds. Equally, the car has inbuilt sensors that allow it to robotically park in tight spaces on the kerbside. I can also buy automated lawnmowers and internet ovens.

Therefore, the chip-based product is becoming hugely pervasive. But banks have so far purely placed chips in traditional

34

products – plastic cards – because of the limitations of traditional thinking. By the mid-2000's banks, led by competition from other industries, are just starting to experiment with other chip-based payment vehicles as discussed, such as the mobile telephone. But here's the most radical concept of payments for the future, and one which is probably only about five years away.

Implant the payment. Stick the chip inside the customer's body. Make the human the payments vehicle.

You may think that is idiotic, but when do you ever see anyone on the *Star Trek* series pay for anything? Unless everything in the future is free, what is taking place? The fact is that the Trekkies are all paying through invisible, wireless, chip-enabled human interactions.

Invisible payments

Here's the idea.

Chip-based products become really powerful within the next five years, as powerful as a laptop in 2000. As a result, the chip is offered as an implant for anyone to use in one of four applications.

The first is as a health monitor. The chip automatically senses and tracks blood pressure, cholesterol, brain activity and heart rate continually 24 hours a day, and wirelessly sends this to a base station in the automated home. The base station reports any unusual or suspicious changes in these parameters to your doctor should strange activity occur. This guarantees that early indications of anything like a stroke or heart attack are caught before you would even have thought there was a problem.

Equally, because the chip is monitoring your heart, brain and blood, should the chip be removed from the body, it becomes null and void. Hence, the chip is always guaranteed to only be operating as long as the human owner of the chip has it implanted.

As a result, the second usage is for immigration and identification purposes. Instead of passports and identification cards, governments rapidly move towards the promotion of chip implants to provide fast and convenient travel services:

No more heavy duty and intrusive searches at airports, ports and terminals, just turn up and go. For citizens who have the National Chip ID, you can just go through the wireless fast track station and hop on your boat, plane or train ... meanwhile, for the rest of you, please join the 30-minute queue for the security scan, take off your shoes, belts and jewellery and ensure that your pacemaker is switched off.

I know many folks would jump at the chance of such a fast track system, even if it meant having a small chip implanted in your arm.

Another reason I would have such a chip implanted would be for location services, which is our third application of the chip implant. Just as we chip our dogs and cats so that, should they become road kill, the vet can identify who the deceased belongs to, so we will chip ourselves so that our loved ones and family can track down where we are. This is partly due to our own concerns over security and terrorism, but also in order to enable us to be found if we are lost or if we just want our family to be reassured we are ok during travels overseas. This is also not so far-fetched, as many people already chip their children, just that the chips are not implanted. They are in telephones and we use GSM tracking to find out where they are. Now, various firms manufacturing shoes are offering chip-implanted shoes so that you can do the same without your child knowing! Soon, chip-based location services will become standard and the idea of having one inside is going to be the most reassuring way for a parent to track their child as, unlike shoes and telephones, such chips cannot be lost or dumped whilst doing other mischievous activities.

This leads to our fourth application. If chip implants enable us to be guaranteed health, security and ease of travel, why not use the same services as Payments: the Next Generation?

An implanted chip would enable people to pay in exactly the same way as we are thinking of payments for mobile and contactless, it is purely a small step forward to use chip implants for payments. After all, it is all still chip-based, just that the chip is now much more powerful and usable for multiple applications. The chip is now meeting government and society needs for security, health and safety, so why would a bank not use this capability?

How would it work?

In order to illustrate how the process would work in practice, let us use the example of John Jones.

John is a hardworking man with a complex multi-channel financial account with Acme Bank. John has signed up for the National Chip ID program and, in order to get his chip implanted, has handed in his driving licence and passport. All of this information is now part of his wireless chip information. He has visited his local doctor's practice, and his doctor has wirelessly enabled the health application to start the health monitoring services of blood pressure, heart rate and brain activity. John has also signed up with "TrackIt" services who can let his wife and parents know his location within 200 metres anywhere on the planet ... as long as John has his open broadcast enabled. This is a facility which is purely for user's discretion where the TrackIt service can be switched on and off dependent upon what your family needs to know. Nevertheless, if the police want to override the user's broadcast block, then they can. Finally, John has arrived at Acme Bank and has asked them to enable his payments service.

Acme's wireless application has already identified John and verified his details with the government's national identity database. As a result, they purely switch on the "wireless payments" service related to his unique chip identification, in the same way that they would have done for his mobile RFID or SIM chip, or his EMV contactless card.

John is now free to leave the bank and start making invisible wireless payments. His first port of call is therefore to the electrical store to buy Apple's latest release of iGod, where users are able to control everything in their house using a simple iPod style control panel. The branding had been questionable, but Steve Jobs was powerful enough to ignore such challenges.

The iGod, priced at $5,000 – a 95% mark-up – is a pretty sizeable purchase and John is keen to see if his new Acme wireless payments service will work. Therefore, as he picks up his order, he sees the store's payments screen flash up "Payment made of $5,000 from debit account John Jones, Acme Bank". John is free to switch this to another account if he actively changes the payment instruction, but he is happy with that payment and walks out of the store all set.

What had happened in terms of the actual payments process, was that as John picked up the iGod at the checkout, the wireless sensors had picked up John's chip signal, indicating a preferred account for payments and had activated the payments process.

These wireless sensors are the same sensors as are already being deployed for NFC payments ... just a bit more powerful.

You may wonder how come John did not need to authorise the payment. The authorisation was the fact that John walked away with the goods without changing any of the instructions. If he had left the goods in-store, no payment would have been taken. If he had actively changed any of the payment instructions by touching the screen, the payment of $5,000 would not have been taken form his preferred deposit account. The fact John took the goods and did not change the payment method, meant the payment was taken and made wirelessly without any authentication or further identification required.

In terms of John himself needing to provide identification, no identification or authentication is required because the system is just looking for the chip to be live. The fact the chip is enabled and live is good enough. The chip does not work if it is removed from John's body. Furthermore, the chip is monitoring John's heart, brain and blood and knows there is no change of situation and that he is alive. The system knows John is therefore not being robbed or mugged or forced to make a payment he does not want to make because he is calm, alive and the system knows that it can only be him ... so why would you need any other identification or authentication?

No biometric, no PIN, no signature, no nothing. Just simple, wireless, convenient, seamless payments. As easy as breathing.

That is the future of payments.

The future of payments

The future described in this paper is not that far away. For example, the conceptual outline shown above is actually already implemented. OK, only in quirky little nightclub in Barcelona right now, but it is already here. You may retort that it's still implying something far too intrusive and wacky for any bank to contemplate as well.

The idea of customers having "Intel Inside"? Ludicrous.

But some people thought the same about people using telephones outside. Many people thought that mobile telephones were only for rich idiots when they first came out, but now virtually everyone on the planet has one, or access to one.

Only a few years ago, many people did not believe that MP3 players would succeed. Who would want to mess around getting music off their PC? Then the iPod became a multi-billion dollar global market that rescued Apple.

In 2004, a group of payment professionals told me that mobile payments were about 10 to 20 years away and would only succeed when a Wal-Mart or Virgin launched the service. Two years later, PayPal Mobile was launched and, within a few months, mobile payment pilot programs were everywhere.

Customers with "Intel inside" are going to be used in a number of pilot applications by 2010, will be noticeable by 2015 and common by 2020.

Chip implants will become common if and for no other reason than it makes sense. It makes sense for national security and cross-border movements. It makes sense for family health and security. It just makes sense. As a result, chip-based invisible payments will become common.

Think about it.

Paper, cardboard and plastic as identification with passwords, identification numbers and fingerprints is all so ... it is all so ... so 20th century.

All of the areas described in this paper – contactless, mobile, biometric payments – are therefore just the transient evolutions of the information revolution and the networked world. They are here today and gone tomorrow, just like the Dodo. The final outcome of the world's latest revolution in commerce will be chip-based, wirelessly transmitted invisible payments. And gradually, the 5,000 year old coin, the 200 year old cheque book and the 50 year old plastic card, will disappear.

After all, when do you ever see them being used in *Star Trek*?

Chapter 2 Mobile payments: a vision of the future

Introduction

Back in 2003, a group of American bankers were asked to estimate when mobile payments would take off. Most of them said: "not in our lifetime". Then, in May 2007, these bankers were faced with the launch of the first major mobile banking service from Bank of America. They probably laughed that off too, although that service attracted over two and half million active users within two years, representing a third of all mobile banking users in the US. Just goes to show that if you want a vision of the future, don't ask a banker.

Mobile payments: the battleground of the future (2009)

Thomas Bostrøm Jørgensen, CEO of mobile payments and financial solutions firm Luup, presented at the Financial Services Club the other day. He spun an interesting story, particularly around the tripartite models emerging of mobile financial services, where they are either bank-led, carrier-led or a bank-carrier partnership. The latter is probably harder than the other models, as it means co-operating and most firms want to 'own the customer' (I really hate that phrase – no-one 'owns' me).

According to Thomas, this results in a clear divide between bank-led mobile financial services in the developed economies versus carrier-led mobile financial services in the emerging economies.

That split is interesting as, at some point, the two models will have to come together. The question is how?

Here is a summary of his presentation.

Mobile payments: the battle for the future

There is a battle taking place over supremacy in the mobile payment market. I relish this opportunity to give you some insights on why banks and MNOs can find themselves as opposing parties. And on their chances for success in the battle to dominate the future of mobile payments.

I'm also going to address the commercial issues that arise from contrasting business models. Bank-led models, mobile network operator-led models and the third way, partnership models, can all have their advantages and disadvantages. Experience strongly suggests that different models work differently in different environments, especially when contrasting developed and developing countries.

As all of us here at the FSC have a vested interest in bank-led opportunities, I'm specifically going to talk about whether bank-led mobile payments solutions can succeed in equal measure in both developing and developed countries.

Later, I'll also be sharing with you a sample blueprint for future bank-led roll-outs of mobile payments infrastructure, in the form of a case study from the National Bank of Abu Dhabi.
(…)

Battleground and key protagonists

Now let's remind ourselves of the battleground and key protagonists.

In developed countries mobile banking and payments form only a part of the broader service offering. Most people have a bank account and a mobile phone in these countries, so it is natural that bank-led models should be the norm as banks provide services to their own customers using mobile phones as another delivery channel. Convenience and speed are the key drivers here.

In developing countries by contrast, where much of the population is unbanked but mobile phone penetration is very high, the industry is led by mobile network operators (MNOs).

Their extensive networks of local agents give mobile network operators a clear edge in the battle for control. They can, in fact, often end up operating what amounts to an alternative banking system.

How does it work? One way is through the use of prepaid calling airtime, which performs many of the functions of money and is increasingly a medium of exchange instead of cash. Another way is through stored value accounts where cash is paid onto the phone account and then used for transactions.

As the battle unfolds, we can see that there is also a third way. Banks, MNOs and third-party mobile payments solutions providers can partner to meet customer needs without causing concerns about regulatory matters.

So how are the future demarcations shaping up?

We have all heard that the future of mobile payment could be huge. The world is, after all, expected to have 5 billion mobile phones in action by 2012. (Source: Datamonitor 2008)

But in the battle over who controls that future, many banks are staying on the sideline. And particularly in developing countries, banks aren't winning. It's the MNOs making the most of the opportunity and capturing the revenue.

A business worth fighting for...

(...)

CGAP, the Consultative Group to Assist the Poor, produced a recent survey on financial access. It predicts that the mobile payments market could be worth as much as £365 billion by 2013, with 110 million users in Europe alone by 2014.

By the year 2012, CGAP and the GSM Association estimate there will be 1.7 billion people with a mobile phone but not a bank account. As many as 364 million unbanked people could be reached via branch-less mobile banking.

CGAP estimates that mobile financial services to poor people in emerging economies will increase from nothing to $5 billion in 2012.

Whatever the exact numbers, mobile payments will undoubtedly be an important element in the future of financial services.

MNO-led models

What can be done to shift power structures and get banks more involved? Well the good news for us at the FSC is that the MNO-led model along with strengths also shows weaknesses. Let's look at some:

First of all for competitive reasons most of the MNOs offer the service only to their own customers, thus restricting access and scope.

However, in developing markets the MNO-led mobile payments models are aimed at the very large numbers of unbanked people. The schemes thrive because MNOs have networks of local agents. These handle cash in cash out in far flung areas, far outstripping the local physical presence of banks.

(...)

While it is the networks of agents that give MNOs such a clear advantage, they also expose another issue: the building and maintaining of those networks is a major task..

The relative lack of banking experience can leave MNOs vulnerable though. They could run the risk of being overwhelmed by the success their mobile payments schemes have enjoyed in developing markets.

In countries where registration processes and security measures are not robust, regulators are starting to become concerned about the inroads MNOs-led models are making. Apart from safety of customer money, the potential for money laundering and terrorism financing risks, simple old-fashioned fraud could be an issue.

(...)

Most of you will have heard of the Kenyan example, the M-Pesa mobile payments scheme that passed the 8 million user mark and is largely driven by Vodafone.

But authorities became increasingly concerned that M-Pesa's lack of banking status was a pyramid scheme putting customer funds at risk. And blogs highlighted an article from the East African Standard which concluded that M-PESA "could be a disaster waiting to happen."

(...)

Many other countries still need to address the issues and a clear business opportunity exists for banks to support the efforts and increase their presence. Partnering with banks will give the MNOs additional financial services skills and experience. And will enable banks to diversify revenue generation by accessing un-served segments and growing markets.

But for banks to become more involved they have to go out and forge strategic partnerships. And time is of the essence. The GSMA, the association that represents the interests of the mobile communications industry, is lobbying hard for its members to be allowed to undertake regulated transactions.

Yet in my mind there is no doubt that there is a clear need for banks to add value and be part of developments. And by doing so you could be helping transform Africa's financial economy more than decades of foreign aid have ever achieved.

Bank-led models

In the bank-led model the financial institution holds the stronghold, as the customer account relationship sits with the bank. The bank acts as both the acquirer and issuer. In this model, most common in developed countries, the mobile enables convenient access to transactional and informational services. It is used as a new channel to provide existing banking services or expand services – opening up new levels of efficiency and cost savings, supporting customer retention and acquisition.

Often in the bank-led model, banks focus on informational mobile services, yet the mobile payments arena is opening up new opportunities.

Earlier this year, for example. Deutsche Bank's global transactions banking division announced their plan to offer an instant and secure mobile payments service to banks and corporations in 80 countries. This service does not depend on the mobile network the end-users are on. So no MNO partnerships are needed, they are just providing mobile connectivity services.

Corporate mobile payments in bank-led models

Another approach Luup is pioneering is a lucrative bank-led corporate mobile payments and authorisation solution. This is of interest for banks' corporate customers and their treasurers, particularly corporates with large supply chain distribution networks. Automation has already been a key driver in helping run a more efficient treasury department. But there are even greater, new opportunities by introducing advanced mobile payments solutions.

Why and how?

The ubiquitous reach of smartphones, such as Blackberry, HTC/Android and iPhone, means that treasurers nowadays walk around with the equivalent of a tiny PC in their pocket. Those banks that can leverage this and offer new cost saving functionalities will open up a lucrative market for themselves. New technology enables corporates' end users to make and receive payments, authorise invoices and initiate payments using a company mobile.

In short, new solutions offer real-time payment collection, convenience and the opportunity to reduce operational overhead costs. The opportunities are only just emerging and, again, banks can lead on this.

(...)

Additionally let's not forget the implications of a far-reaching regulatory change in the European payments industry, the Payments Services Directive. The PSD seeks to form an intermediate step between those with and without a credit institution licence. It offers a relatively easy to obtain payments institution licence as of this month, 1st of November to be precise.

This is a great opportunity for non-bank organisations that are keen to have a stake in the mobile payments market. So even in developed markets other entities are now entering the domain of banks.

Partnership models: a Third Way

In an emerging third way, the partnership model, MNOs, banks, NGOs and mobile payments solutions providers seek to collaborate. The entire industry huddles together to create business, drive adoption and acceptance. This takes place mainly in developing countries at present.

Yet negotiations over who has which role are very complex as the value delivered by each party comes under the microscope. Banks need to be clear on their assets, their capabilities and their value before negotiating these partnerships.

The aim is for partners to devise go-to-market strategies that focus on countries rather than individual MNOs or banks. In this model, the activities across the value chain are distributed between partners, which permits them to focus on their core competencies.

In most cases, the MNO provides the network delivering the services to customers and they often also own the customer relationship, data and marketing outreach. The bank tends to look after the funds, the accounts and the Know Your Customer factors in the equation, and retains the responsibility as an acquirer and issuer. They also control the regulatory aspect.

This model can help financial institutions reach new target markets, increasing their revenue.

However, the issues you want to be aware of with this model include potential conflicts around customer interaction and ownership. Both parties are keen to maintain the interaction with the customer for purposes of retention, cross- and up-sell. Then there are potential issues around revenue sharing; and who owns the float? And what about the lucrative exchange commission in the case of international remittances? Finally, cooperation can also be a challenge when each stakeholder is keen to imprint their own brand and marketing on the new payment system.

Another challenge is the fact that MNOs main interest in a highly competitive mobile market tends to be customer retention, rather than revenue generation from mobile payments services themselves. While for banks, new customer and revenue generation has to be top of the agenda when penetrating developing markets with little banking infrastructure.

So the future still holds many challenges. Yet I believe that banks can work with MNOs and also help to reassure regulators. By successfully tackling the concerns, all parties could help reshape the future in developing countries.

And it is vital all parties are committed to making this work 'first time right' in developing countries where there are no alternative transaction infrastructures. If the mobile payment channel is tainted by lack of trust or reliability as a result of cutting corners, there is no alternative channel for financial services delivery to fall back on.

It is a huge challenge. But one which could be very rewarding.

Money for Nothing and your Cheques for Free

Blueprint for the future

You've heard about the different models. What about taking a look at a successful bank-lead implementation, to show a possible path to the future?

There is no such thing as a standard roll-out. Each country requires a different approach.

Earlier I briefly referred to our partnership with the National Bank of Abu Dhabi in the UAE. The UAE is an interesting example at it has some of the highest mobile phone ownership figures in the world. One recent study from the Arab Advisors Group shows penetration in UAE at nearly 200 per cent. (Source: Telecommunications Regulatory Authority, 2008)

So here is a sample blueprint for future bank-led mobile payments roll-outs. The bank has set up Arrow, an SMS-based payments service. This allows NBAD account holders, prepaid card holders and salary card holders to send money to anyone in the UAE with a mobile phone.

The service covers person-to-person money transfer, person-to-merchant bill payments and charity payments. Added to this, the bank has an SMS service for ATM cash-out and is soon rolling out a mobile remittance service. The SMS cash service was the first of its kind, enabling mobile money transfers and ATM cash-out to anyone within the UAE, whether or not they're a registered user of Arrow.

The result of our willingness to tailor the system for the UAE market is an extremely challenging 18-month implementation project. The bank has attempted some things that had never been done before, such as linking a security token to mobile phone transactions, and making mobile transfers available to anyone regardless of whether they are a customer or not.

Security and anti-money laundering issues received particular attention.

Working together, we learned a lot in terms of how much users wanted to transact and what the volumes are like. And once we add cross-border remittance capabilities early next year, we believe the traffic and revenues will increase greatly.

Overall this progressive roll-out is helping to build the business model further for the industry.

Conclusions

What, then, are my principal conclusions about the future potential for the mobile payments market?

At the risk of sounding like an echo of a certain large international mobile network operator, I believe that the future is bright. The future is exciting. The future is challenging. You have the opportunity to help build that future, and improve lives in developing markets as well as make everyday life even easier in developed markets.

But before I begin taking your questions, I would like to end by asking you some of my own.

Have you formulated a long-term strategy in this space?

Are you allocating the resources needed, and do you have people who know enough about the space?

Do you have the technology and the infrastructure?

If someone were to ask you if you would like to reduce costs. And increase operational efficiencies. And tap into new and expanding markets. I'm sure you would answer yes.

Mobile money numbers (2009)

I thought these numbers on mobile money users worth sharing:

♦ The market for mobile applications, or apps, will become "as big as the internet", peaking at 10 million apps in 2020 according to Symbian.

- CGAP produced a recent survey on Financial Access and found that there are 6.2 billion bank accounts worldwide - more than one for every person on the planet - except that 70% of adults in developing countries do not use formal financial services, or are unbanked, compared to 20% of those in developed countries.

- Of the 139 countries that CGAP surveyed, only 40 reported that they encourage or mandate government transfers through the banking system; 14 of these are high-income countries and 10 countries in Latin America. Few countries in other regions are promoting such transfers.

- The survey predicts that the mobile payments market could be worth as much as £365 billion by 2013, with 110 million users in Europe alone by 2014.

- By the year 2012 CGAP and GSMA estimate there will be 1.7 billion people with a mobile phone but not a bank account and as many as 364 million unbanked people could be reached by agent-networked banking through mobile phones.

- CGAP estimate that mobile financial services to poor people in emerging economies will increase from nothing to $5 billion in 2012.

- 40% of Kenyan households have used M-PESA as of late 2008, a figure announced by Caroline Pulver of FSD Kenya as she unveiled the findings of their survey.

- 41% of Filipino mobile money users were able to set up a mobile money account in 5 minutes or less.

- Electronic payments deliver cost savings of at least 1% of a country's GDP when compared to paper, according to Visa.

- Monitise, the mobile money network, has just signed up their millionth customer and are processing 25 million transactions per annum.

More about mobile money (2009)

I'm on holiday and ignoring nearly everything ... almost everything ... but not quite. Just found a couple more links about mobile money that are really interesting so couldn't help but post them.

First, Fast Company has just produced a really good review of all things to do with mobile money:

> "Mobile payments system Boku just announced that it will work with a bevy of social networks and gaming sites. But competitor Zong, was recently chosen to pilot Facebook's virtual currency, called Credits. Both sites will face considerable opposition from Obopay, a seasoned start-up that recently earned the backing of mobile phone giant Nokia for its Nokia Money payment system. Mobile payments are convenient, fast and easy – but which service should you use?"

They go on to look at PayPal and Amazon's TextPayMe, and their answer is that each has its own virtues dependent upon what you are trying to do, e.g. gaming, downloads, sending money, etc. Well worth a view.

The other that caught my eye was the launch of Virgin Mobile's Zoompass in Canada:

> "Virgin Mobile Canada and EnStream LP announced that Virgin Mobile customers can now Zoom each other cash with Zoompass(TM), a groundbreaking new mobile money transfer and payment service. Zoompass is a fast and easy way to send and receive money securely with a mobile phone."

53

Being on hols in a remote place with only a mobile and black-berry to keep in touch means that these things are proving to be of great value.

After all, how else am I going to pay that utility bill I left on the doormat that day I left?

First O2-RBS Visa Cards, now Nokia Obopay Money (2009)

A year ago, I blogged about Royal Bank of Scotland (RBS) announcing the intention to become an MVBO – a Mobile Virtual Banking Operator. The idea is to offer the mechanism for anyone to process mobile payments through the RBS payments system.

The first result of this strategy is the announcement of O2, the mobile carrier, partnering with RBS to offer Visa payment cards in the UK. From small acorns ...

This is not to say that m-payments is just an MVBO space, as the European Payments Council is actively working with the GSM Association to develop standards in this space and other infrastructures, such as Monitise, creating joint ventures with Visa.

But Nokia's press release yesterday announcing that it is working with PayPal is intriguing, to say the least. There's a great quote in there from Mary McDowell, EVP and Chief Development Officer, Nokia:

> "With more than 4 billion mobile phone users and only 1.6 billion bank accounts, global demand for access to financial services presents a strong opportunity to combine mobile devices with simple but powerful financial services such as Nokia Money."

It just makes me wonder whether this means all the handset manufacturers create m-payment systems with Sony Money, iPhone Money (MoBank), and more; and then all the mobile carriers have theirs too with O2 Money, Vodafone Money, T-Mobile Money and more.

If so, there's too many and eventually someone will win out to be the eventual PayPal for Mobile Payments. That's a thought – what are PayPal doing?

Not enough from all I can see. Launched as first mover in 2006, PayPal Mobile has been relatively quiet ever since. Some would say, in fact, that it's going nowhere because they lack a mobile merchant acquirer and the current merchant processing fees are too high for mobile. But don't discount PayPal too fast as they definitely have the brand for this space ... if only they can get the business model to go with it.

Dontcha just love this mobile stuff ...

Mobile payments in China (2009)

Researchers estimate that there were only 83.5 million online payment users in China in 2006, due to the lack of access to payment cards. Admittedly, Tencent with the QQ coin has enabled more payments outside the banking system, but the lack of access to e-payments has been an inhibitor to the democratisation of commerce in China.

However, this is changing and changing fast with UMPay, a Joint Venture between Unionpay and China Mobile, targeting this space through mobile services.

According to UMPay, e- and m- payment users will exceed 500 million people next year and there are already 100 million m-payment users under the UMPay scheme. That's more than the total number of online payment users only two years ago.

UMPay launched in 2003 and provides China Mobile users with a comprehensive mobile payment platform and mobile payment system provide mobile wallets, financial message services, top-ups and mobile ticketing.

Money for Nothing and your Cheques for Free

Where they are going to gain the greatest growth is from rural farmers though. This is the strategy of UMPay today – to saturate the rural locations with UMPay access – and will take the 100 million users through the half a billion number in the very near future according to UMPay CEO Bin Zhang.

Mobile finance is fast demonstrating its power in countries that are using such technologies to leapfrog established financial infrastructures.

In China's case, this is a sophisticated mobile financial service from billing and payments to utilities and transportation. In other words, a comprehensive use of mobile for banking and financial services.

We could learn a thing or two.

Mobile payment provider 'infuriates' banks (2009)

I've blogged a few times about M-Pesa. The first time was in late 2007, when Citibank did a deal to roll the M-Pesa model worldwide for remittances. Then again in 2008, when Royal Bank of Scotland (RBS) announced the idea of a business model based upon being an MBNO, a Mobile Banking Network Operator.

The idea of the latter is that you take the model of Vodafone in Kenya with M-Pesa, which is managed by their subsidiary Safaricom, and link the MVNO (Vodafone) with the MBNO (RBS) to offer mobile payments in any country of choice.

When RBS told me their plans to do this, they stated that it was because Vodafone had become the largest bank in Kenya by accident and, as this was not a core activity for them, it made sense to team up and have a bank manage this non-core activity.

This may well be true, but now M-Pesa is at the centre of a storm of controversy.

As banks have seen how successful they have become, they have become more angry about the service. The whole thing spilled over into a full-scale row just before Christmas, when headlines ran such as this one from the Nairobi Star: "Big Banks in Plot to Kill M-Pesa".

Oh dear. What had M-Pesa done wrong?

The newspaper reports that: "Four big local banks have formed an 'ad hoc committee' to try and get M-Pesa stopped. The bankers pitched their case to Michuki (the Kenyan Finance Minister) at dinner on Monday, 8th December. They argued that M-Pesa was similar to a 'pyramid scheme' and that people could lose their money if it collapsed."

Aha! A Bernie Madoff-style Ponzi scheme, eh? Shut it down.

The accusation is that rogue agents dealing with M-Pesa payments are skimming off the top and stealing the cash.

I suspect the real reason is that, as the article reports later, the M-Pesa service was launched in March 2007 with the blessing of the Kenyan government and "now has over 5,000,000 registered users and almost 5,000 registered outlets. It has transferred almost KES60 billion (around US$765 million) since it started. In September M-Pesa transferred KES9.61 billion (US$120 million) and in October reportedly over KES10 billion."

The bankers' pressure on the Finance Minister obviously had some effect as, after Christmas, the newspapers reported that M-Pesa could be a "disaster waiting to happen" due to the lack of an appropriate regulatory structure.

The storm rages on this week as papers say that the service must now be brought under the regulatory system of the National Bank of Kenya, and that their agent-based model is open to unscrupulous practices, which is where the whole pyramid scheme dialogue starts.

There may be some gist to the issues and reasons why the service needs to change, but surely it's better to have a simple money

Money for Nothing and your Cheques for Free

transfer service using mobile telephones than having to pay taxi drivers a fortune to move money between villages physically.

And where were the banks when this service was being started? Just looking at the high net worth client base, I suspect.

For all its foibles, M-Pesa is a brilliant innovation and yes, the agents needs to be monitored and the service regulated, but whatever you do, don't break an innovation that works, Mr. Michuki.

M-billing: a killer app? (2008)

I had a fascinating chat today with the head of payments at one of the largest British utility firms. She was frustrated by the fact that they cannot switch standing order customers over to direct debits. For those unfamiliar, standing orders are a payment type in the UK where the accountholder typically sets up a monthly transfer of funds to another account. Like a direct debit, but the other way around, e.g. the payer creates the order rather than the payee. The difference is that many folks create standing orders and forget about them. They just pay a set amount per month and they don't switch them off. This was her frustration. In fact, in some cases, the payers had a monthly standing order instruction and a direct debit so the firm got paid twice by the payer. Lucky old utility firm.

The problem is that standing orders cost, and so they want to switch these guys across to direct debit only. However, the utility cannot close a standing order instruction. Only the payer can do that and, in many instances, these are older customers who are unaware or too infirm to change the payment process. So she's stuck with the problem of keeping up with accepting standing orders, even though it's less than 1% of all of her payment types and is darned annoying as a result.

Mind you, we often find we open new channels but cannot close old ones. Just look at cheques!

On the other hand, she was excited about one new channel, mobile payments, and particularly the potential of m-billing. Bearing in mind this is a corporate client, this could therefore be a killer app for the banks.

M-billing for direct debits that alert each time a regular payment instruction, such as utility bills, is processed makes great sense, as the customer can immediately see the payment and the bill in real-time. No hanging around for an email saying, "here's your bill and click here to look at it". Just an alert that says, "your monthly £50 payment for electricity will be processed tomorrow – just click to see your bill or statement".

This corporate client believes this offers huge potential as the user can see their billing, their payment instruction and any other information related to billing, and query, authorise or change details in real-time. No messing about.

The result? M-billing appears to be another killer app for mobile, and seems to be far better received than eBPP or similar internet-based billing approaches.

Chapter 3 The Paypal story

Introduction

PayPal is a real conundrum for bankers. On the one hand, they could have and should have built and deployed a PayPal system themselves. On the other, having missed that opportunity, they should have acquired PayPal before eBay did. Failing in both counts, it's not become a bit of a monster and, in ten short years, has achieved a third of the size of Citigroup's Payments business just by processing small transactions on the internet. But PayPal does more than that and is probably the most dramatic shift in transaction processing for finance since credit cards were invented.

Why PayPal et al REALLY matter! (2010)

So I've argued that PayPal and their brethren of social monies don't matter. It was like unleashing the sceptical banker that I know resides deep within me, and it felt good.

Then I got a dose of new reality vision (maybe due to so many comments on yesterday's piece – see below) and it felt not so good, because PayPal and their brethren really do matter. In fact, they matter a lot more than we think.

Most of their secret lies in the pages of the innovator's dilemma. The premise is that a new operator enters your industry offering something that looks irrelevant; before you know it, the irrelevant operators subsumes you and the industry by changing its economic paradigms. The best example is Japanese car operators in the US in the 1950s who offered cheap new cars. Ford and GM thought they were rust buckets and dismissed them as such. However, Americans could suddenly buy new cars and they did en masse. The second hand car market disappeared and, over the years, the Japanese car manufacturers upscaled and produced cheap luxury cars. After half a century, Ford and GM were on their knees and the Japanese had won.

This central tenet of theory is absolutely critical when we look at PayPal, Facebook credits, Twitpay and more, as these developments will be a dilemma for banks, in the innovator's dilemma style. The question is: do the bankers see the threat?

First, PayPal and their clan are not thinking about being the cream or froth on the cake. They are, instead, thinking about a new market dedicated to froth and cream that has nothing to do with cakes. Whilst bankers focus upon cake, PayPal and the new breed of payments processors are focusing upon cream. They have recognised that customers don't want boring old stodgy cakes, but flexible sweet products that can go with cakes, meringues, biscuits, crumbles and even drinks: think cappuccino!

So they are creating a whole new market for cream, or rather payments, that has nothing to do with traditional processing but sits alongside it today, and could replace it tomorrow.

This new payments market is focused upon convenience, fun and the socialisation of money, rather than on the payments process or the need to pay. This is why it is so different – it's the virtualisation of exchanging credits – and so yes, it is frictionless, flexible and free. More than this, it's different.

Second, just like the car industry of the 1950s, it's also insignificant as a dilemma right now. As mentioned before, PayPal are processing peanuts – $72 billion of transactions – compared to banks that process $4 trillion per day ... but give it time and you have to inevitably ask:

When do we take this market seriously? When it gets to a trillion dollars a year? A trillion a month? A trillion a day?

You see, PayPal are moving and extending reach into higher ticket items and into core merchant services. And what happens if and when PayPal offer a cashback program? Oh, yes ... they already do.

So what would happen if PayPal started offering real incentives, as in undercutting banks if you use a PayPal account as your core payments account, rather than paying via card or withdrawing into a bank account?

They could easily do this, as PayPal don't allow negative balances, and are rumoured to hold over a billion dollars in deposits on accounts at any time. That's a significant figure to play with as a float.

Third, and most important, who owns the last mile? This is the most critical question, and was raised in yesterday's comments. After all, if your main interface to monetary movements becomes PayPal or Facebook, so much so that you forget that a bank or bank account exists behind that brand, then does anything behind it matter?

So here's the long-term play. PayPal becomes your primary interface to money. After a while, using their banking licence, PayPal gains direct access to the electricity generators of monetary movement – the clearing, settlement and payments infrastructures of the world.

They move upscale from being peanuts processing for consumers to displacing acquiring and issuing banks from the payments process through an ever-expanding range of services:

♦   PayPal for Merchant Services

♦   PayPal for Working Capital

♦   PayPal for Supply Chain Finance

♦   PayPal for Trade Finance

♦   PayPal for Trading

♦   PayPal for NYSE

♦   PayPal for the London Stock Exchange

PayPal for ANYTHING!

By the way, it's not just PayPal at this point of time, but any firm that wants to operate in the cream and froth market.

At this point, you've realised the innovator's dilemma. What started as insignificant small beans payments that appears to be froth or cream on your cake, has suddenly become core business services and major margin erosion as the new entrants upscale and redefine the model. The payments businesses erode and are substituted by new markets services.

To be clear, if you remember that PayPal currently generates around $800 million in revenue per quarter, or $3 billion a year, then compare this with today's other big boys. The world's largest global transaction processors, such as Citibank, typically generate around $10 billion in revenues and $3 billion+ in profits.

So today, Citibank's transaction services is three times bigger than PayPal. In 2002, PayPal's annual revenues were around $200 million. In 2005, they broke a billion. Today, they've reached three billion. They're growing at an average of over 25% per annum. And they can keep growing as they expand services and upscale.

What will inexorably happen is that the core of the payments world – the infrastructures, settlement systems and clearing houses – will remain. These do not need to be substituted, as it's just cables and pipework. But like the electricity and water companies, it's the owner of the interaction and therefore, the customer, that is key and will change. The owner of the 'last mile', as we refer to them.

And that's where our creamy new players are making their froth. You see they enjoy being the cream on the cake because they are defining two separate markets – exchanging virtual credits in a digital world versus making a payment.

In conclusion, PayPal and their brethren matter because they are redefining payments and may be insignificant today ... but tomorrow?

Money for Nothing and your Cheques for Free

Meanwhile, bankers can cry: 'Let them eat cake' ... trouble is, what happens when no-one wants cake anymore?

Why PayPal et al don't matter (2010)

Many of us get excited about new and different toys in the payments world.

From Jack Dorsey's Twittering, through Square to PayPal's billions of payments, we think the world is changing dramatically. SMS texting payments in Africa and credit exchanges on Facebook add weight to our arguments for change in the core of bank processing.

We then use these illustrations of small change to make allegations about big change. We speculate that everyone will be using Twitter for payments via PayPal's core system within the next few years, for example. I do it myself because it's nice to see a bit of concern in a banker's eye; a slightly less confident swagger in a global transaction processor; a jitter of confidence in a commercial banker's pricing. But it's all just a bit of noise when you look at the reality of these systems. It's just cream on the cake.

In fact, I would say that all of the online P2P consumer developments in payments are nothing more than a wart on the backside of the flea attached to the hairs on the backside of the cat, which purrs in the lap of the banker who operates just a small piece of the parts of the whole, that comprise today's global payments industry.

Oh yes, and that backside's wart includes PayPal. Shock, horror, heresy but yes, it is nothing special. PayPal, Facebook Credits, Square ... even prepaid cards and mobile payments, it's all just a little bit of froth or cream on the layers of the cake of the core banking industry, and its heart of payments processing.

Let me illustrate it best by picking on PayPal (sorry, mates). Today, PayPal deals with around $80 billion worth of transactions per annum – they broke $20 billion in transactions processed for the first time in Q4 2009, processing $21.4 billion in transactions for a revenue of $795.6 million. That sounds significant, doesn't it?

For them it is, as PayPal is a major growth machine that has eaten its parent, eBay, by becoming the de facto standard for on-line payments. PayPal's revenues hit a billion per year in 2005 – now they do that per quarter. The thing is that it is major for them but, in the scheme of the overall payments world, it's not major at all.

First, their revenues are peanuts. Assuming PayPal generates around $3 billion per annum in revenues this year, it's still a long way off the largest banks that make $3 billion in pure profit in a typical year.

Second, PayPal sits on top of the core banking infrastructure. It hasn't created anything new. It's just added a layer of cream to the cake of payments. It sits on top of Visa and MasterCard which, in turn, sit on top of bank accounts. So nothing has changed. This is why PayPal is cream on the cake, but not a core ingredient.

The core ingredients are the infrastructures of clearing houses and banks, of counterparty systems and SWIFT messaging, of Real-Time Gross Settlement and Card Processing systems. Pay-Pal is just a little bit of cream on those layers of cake. For this reason, although I love PayPal as a model of providing payments for new internet and mobile services, from a payments context it is nothing serious.

As for Facebook Credits or other add-on services like Twit-pay, which all use PayPal as their underlying service, these are just froth on the cream.

Third, even if you take them seriously, what are they actually doing? They're providing a bit of payment functionality on top of the card and bank account functionality. Actually no, they're

Money for Nothing and your Cheques for Free

not even providing that. What they're actually providing is a bit of account aggregation of payments for a small fee. In other words, because banks and payments processors aren't interested in sub-$10 payments processing, someone had to do it and that someone was PayPal. So PayPal scooped up all of these P2P small payments online, and that's their core business. It's not high value payments processing. It's peanuts processing.

OK, so PayPal does the odd airline ticket for $1,000 but, for every airline ticket, they process thousands more dollars for buying cables, DVDs, mobile phone covers and similar goods at $10 or less. Bring on Facebook credits and Twitpay and they're processing $100s of more dollars for sharing a note, reading a page or downloading a song for $0.99 or less. In other words, they are just payments aggregation services.

Like a telephone billing service, PayPal and its gang of payments aggregators offer small payments processing on a massively scalable platform. By doing this, it enables them to generate enough to warrant a worthwhile bank payment per month. But they are not payments processing, just aggregating payments like a telephone service.

A telephone service provider processes hundreds of transactions a month to generate a single worthwhile monthly payment through the banking system. PayPal, Facebook and Twitpay are doing the same thing for online services. This is why they are actually irrelevant, in terms of core payments processing.

Core payments processing represents $4 trillion of debit and credit card payments per annum, significantly more than PayPal's $72 billion for the year. Core payments represents the almost $4 trillion in foreign exchange transactions performed every day. That's over a quadrillion dollars worth of transactions per year. A quadrillion dollars per annum makes PayPal look like a bit of detritus on the landscape of global payments volumes.

This is not to say that PayPal is detritus. It's important, but it is not the be-all and end-all of innovation or even change because, when it comes to payments, nothing much has changed. In fact, banks are starting to eat back into their business by launching secure online payments systems like iDeal and Rightcliq by Visa. And this is easy, when you have an industry that processes gazillions of dollars per year using standards, structures and systems which have globally stood the test of time. These standards, structures and systems allow the billions of transactions in global capital markets and corporate supply chain and person-to-person payments to operate.

These are the core ingredients of the cake.So yes, add to this a little bit of cream on the cake, PayPal; or add to this a little froth on the cream, Facebook and Twitpay.

But don't mistake the froth and cream as core.

It's not.

PayPal does have competition (2009)

I've talked about how PayPal is not as pally as they used to be. Some might say that this is because they are the last man standing in the last-chance saloon of online payments, but that is not true. There's always new competition.

In fact, a year ago, I talked about one big new competitor in the form of Amazon. Amazon's checkout service was offered to anyone as a simple drop and click payments app to plug into their website. So how's it going? Well, apparently.

According to website Amazon Strategies, Checkout by Amazon, or CBA for short, is offered by over 300 retailers, with several of the top 500 internet retailers using this as their preferred payments tool including:

- Toolking.com – a company that does some great work with social networking and has some innovative micro sites like Tooliday.com;
- Patagonia – a manufacturer that sells direct and via retailers like REI, Dick's Sporting Goods, etc; and
- Jockey – a manufacturer that sells direct.

The comment Amazon Strategies makes is how successful they are doing with online distribution for manufacturers who want to sell direct, and there "are lots of manufacturers that want to sell direct to consumers".

Too darned right.

Maybe that's why some of the big heavyweights in our digital planet are getting into payments, with Apple rumoured to be offering iTunes accounts as a method of payment for digital downloads on third party websites.

Similarly, Facebook has often been mooted as thinking about getting into more commercial activities, such as extending their credit system to online payments, as have Twitter.

All in all, PayPal does have competition so they're not alone out there. But, historically, they've always managed to keep ahead of the competition. We shall see what happens this time if, and when, the big heavyweights take them on.

PayPal not so pally (2009)

I've written a fair bit of positive stuff about PayPal over the last few years, and was intrigued by two headlines today.

One, "PayPal reported me to the FBI".

Two, "PayPal up charges to customers ... and don't tell them".

The first is blogger Ghetto Webmaster, who posted an image of PayPal's logo to illustrate how phishing works in January 2008. Mid-July 2009, he receives an email from PayPal via his ISP, threatening legal action for the misuse of the PayPal logo in a potential phishing scam and violating their trademarks. Oh yes, and they also told the FBI about it, just in case.

Ghetto Webmaster responded by asking his ISP to "please tell eBay/PayPal Inc to p**s off" and by writing a new blog entry about it, copied to PayPal via email with the message "congrats on making your company look like a bunch of retards".

Very constructive. What he didn't expect is that the blogging community would show who the retard was, when Mr. Webmaster received this message: "I'm an email scammer and thanks to you hosting that image, now I can send out as many phishing emails as I want. All I have to do is link that image to my phishing site and plenty of morons will click it."

Kerching!

Oh yes, and as we're talking about ringing up money for nothing, the other big headline of the day (with almost 3,000 diggs already) is that PayPal have started charging customers for goods or services a fee of 2.9% plus 30 cents per transaction for payments that used to be free. This is big news because they didn't bother to tell their customers they were doing this. PayPal's PR manager, Charlotte Hill, said: "We didn't want to make a huge formal communication out of this pricing change, because we weren't really adding any fees, and we were hoping it would be a more useful experience for people."

What was Ghetto Webmaster saying about retards?

PS: I got an email from PayPal in response to this post, saying that they had changed the way they charged for the service in the UK a year ago, and sent an email to all PayPal UK customers saying as much. Was it this experience that caused them not tell their US customers, I wonder?

PayPal's 10th anniversary (2008)

I wrote an in-depth analysis about PayPal's 100 months birthday 18 months ago, and now they're celebrating their official 10th anniversary so I thought I would add a small addendum. Although I say it's a small addendum, it's quite an interesting one.

Basically, I was updating some old slides about PayPal and thought that I should track their number of users over the years, as they do publish these numbers. First of all, I looked up the last published quarterly results from PayPal on the eBay website.

In their latest company presentation, published June 16th, they have these figures:

- PayPal operates in 190 markets using 17 currencies;

- A third of people in the UK have a PayPal account;

- Over 100,000 websites accept PayPal in Europe.

PayPal has more users than most payment services:

- PayPal   141 million *

- Chase   115 million

- Citi   114 million

- AMEX   78 million

- CapitalOne   59 million

- Discover Card   50 million

Total Payment Volume (TPV) grew by a third in 2007 to $47 billion.

In their Q1 2008 results, eBay state: "PayPal had a strong quarter with $582 million in net revenue, an increase of 32% year-over-year. Net total payment volume (TPV) for the quarter was $14.42 billion, an increase of 34% year-over-year.

*164 million according to Q1 2008 results

The net revenue and net TPV growth was driven primarily by the continued strong

growth of Merchant Services globally and increased penetration on eBay internationally. Growth in global active accounts increased to 60.2 million, representing 17% year-over-year growth. Globally, PayPal will continue to focus on greater penetration into the Marketplaces business and the acquisition of new merchants."

In my own research, I found that PayPal's accounts grew as follows:

	Users (millions)	YoY % rise	Active accounts (millions)	YoY % rise	% Active accounts to users
Q1 2000	1				
Q1 2001	7	700			
Q1 2002	14	100			
Q1 2003	27	93			
Q1 2004	46	70			
Q1 2005	72	57	22		30
Q1 2006	105	46	29	32	28
Q1 2007	153	46	36	24	24
Q1 2008	164	7	60	67	37
CAGR	89.17%		28.5%		

What this shows is the phenomenal 89% CAGR rise of a firm since its founding in December 1998, although this CAGR slowed in the last three years to just 25%. That's still good by many standards, but nowhere near as good as it used to be.

Maybe that's the reason why PayPal now focuses upon active accounts rather than registered users. An active account is defined as a user who sent or received at least one payment through PayPal during the last quarter, and it's an amazing number to focus upon, when you see that PayPal's active accounts almost doubled in the last year. This is what accounts for the spike to 28.5% CAGR in active accounts, a far more interesting number.

Why?

Money for Nothing and your Cheques for Free

Well, what made the active users double?

Looking at the numbers in more depth, it's not the revenue or total payment volume (TPV):

	Q1 2008	Q1 2007	Q1 2006	Q1 2005
Net revenue	$582m	$439m	$335.1m	$233.1m
Net TPV	$14.42bn	$11.36bn	$8.8bn	$6.2bn
Global active accounts	60.2m	35.9m	29.2m	22.1m
Total accounts	164m	153.1m	105m	71.6m

Or try that a different way. Instead of quarters, what about by year:

	2004 (year)	2007 (year)
Net revenue	$698m	$1,900m
Net TPV	$18.9bn	$47bn
Global active accounts	20.1m	57m
Total accounts	63.8m	158m
Countries	45	190

Ah. From 45 to 190 countries in the last three years. Maybe that's the secret.

Comparing 2006 and 2007:

	2006 (millions)	2007 (millions)
Total accounts	133.0	158
Active accounts	37.6	57
Total Payment Volume	$37,752	$47,874

Yep. That $10 billion annual increase in TPV shows a spike, as does the increase in countries and active accounts.

I realise that these numbers use different time periods for comparison but, overall, I reckon that the mixture of innovations, such as becoming a bank in Europe and offering mobile payments as a first mover, to expanding across borders and territories worldwide, is the secret behind PayPal's success. This has allowed them to grow the franchise, reach more people, be more appealing across more channels, and offer more currencies across more countries than almost any other payments provider.

That's PayPal's secret to success. Along with viral marketing that means folks send messages saying "you've got money" ... that makes most folks open a PayPal account.

This is not to say that PayPal is it. There's plenty of competition around. First, there are the big internet competitors to PayPal, such as Google CheckOut and Amazon's Flexible Payment Services. Second is a whole raft of other pretenders, such as Alert Pay, WorldPay, PayFlow, LinkPoint, Authorize.Net, Nochex, 2Check-Out, or PayByCheck. Third are the big regional players, such as Alipay in China, owned by Alibaba.

And then there are battles that PayPal is entering into as they expand their own franchise, such as the deferred payment service, "Pay Later", which competes with CIT Bank's "Bill Me Later".

So times may be good for PayPal, but they are still being just as challenged by competitors a decade on as they were in 1998.

A fascinating firm to watch, and a fascinating space to be in.

Celebrating PayPal's Centenary (2007)

(extracted from a white paper authored by Chris Skinner.)

What? PayPal 100 years old – surely not?

Well no. PayPal's not 100 years old. In a remarkably understated way though, which no-one noticed – not even PayPal – PayPal is celebrating a milestone.

In March 2007, PayPal celebrated being 100 months old. Yes, the upstart firm with only 133 million users and more merchants than Visa, MasterCard and American Express combined, is just 100 months old.

It is a mere child. Younger than MacAuley Caulkin in *Home Alone*, and just a bit older than Drew Barrymore when she starred in *E.*, PayPal is striking way above its weight ... striking fear in some bankers' hearts and hope in the social revolution of the internet age.

But what is PayPal really all about, why does it work the way it does and where is it going in the future? I was lucky enough to find out by visiting PayPal's UK Headquarters to get an update on PayPal Mobile, PayPal Europe and PayPal worldwide, so here's the low-down.

(...)

Why PayPal works

PayPal works for three major reasons.

The first reason was timing, as Max Levchin and Peter Thiel (the founders) saw that there was no way to support person-to-person buying and selling on the internet during 1998. As a result, they switched their focus from the failed ventures supporting payments using handheld devices to making payments using the internet in 1998.

Back then, less than a decade ago, most internet commerce was still based upon traditional payment systems using cheques and money orders. Even eBay was fuelled by payments made by regular land mail back then.

That is not to say that there were not online payments trials taking place at the time. For example, there was a lot of marketing flurry over firms such as Beenz and Flooz. The trouble was that people did not trust these payment systems because they were new and were flawed because they were not trusted as real currencies.

PayPal had a few vital differences:

◆   It used the dollar as its medium of exchange, rather than trying to create a new currency for online payments;

- ◆ It used email for communications; and
- ◆ It used the existing bank networks for making the payment.

(...)

The fact that PayPal relied on tried and trusted methods of exchange – the US dollar and the banking networks – meant that it rapidly became accepted and used online.

This is the first critical factor.

The second is the viral nature of PayPal or, as it is sometimes referred to, the network effect. The network effect is true of telephones, fax machines and computers where each one added to the network has a 'squaring' effect, as in it doubles the power of the network.

(...)

With the internet, each user creates a squared effect because the internet is two-way, not one-way. The internet can receive, like a TV, but also send. Therefore, three PCs on the network become nine rather than three, because of this squared effect. In other words, the networked effect enables nine variations of communication between the three devices: PC1 to PC2 and PC3, PC2 to PC1 and PC3, and PC3 to PC1 and PC2. It is not just another dumb device on the network, but an interacting, intelligent point of communication. The next user makes it 16 possibilities, or 4^2, because they can now all interact with each other. It's not just another one-way device.

This squared network effect is the very nature of the age of interacting and socialising online, and is a core reason why PayPal took off as quickly as it did. For example, as you gain each user they become a viral marketer for PayPal. And viral marketing, as we now know, is one of the critical factors firms are trying to exploit on the internet today, but seven years ago, few people had got this message.

(...)

Nevertheless, PayPal was still just a fledgling and there were many other contenders around at the time, apart from Beenz and Flooz, such as eBay's Billpoint and Amazon's Accept. Equally, the banking industry had not sat on their hands, as Citibank had launched c2it with AOL and MSN, BankOne had emonyemail, and Western Union had BidPay.

So how did PayPal beat all of these established names?

They achieved this through the final success factor, which is the most critical factor in building PayPal's business. They made online payments cheap by minimising the cost of transactions and authentication.

(...)

The result of being based upon banking services and offering the lowest cost per transaction through emailed payments established PayPal's business model. The promotion, marketing and 'network effect' then turbo-charged PayPal to become the de factor standard for online payments.

(...)

PayPal in Europe

One of the really interesting things is how PayPal has expanded its footprint around the world, and especially in Europe. For example:

- PayPal has offices in 15 countries outside the US, including the UK, Canada, Australia, Austria, Belgium, France, Germany, Italy, Spain, Ireland, the Netherlands, Switzerland and China.

- PayPal has offices in 15 countries but operates in 103 – virtually the whole world, in other words.

- PayPal operates 17 currencies including US Dollars, Canadian Dollars, Australian Dollars, Euros, Pounds Sterling, Japanese Yen, Chinese RMB, Czech Koruna, Danish Krone, Hong Kong Dollar, Hungarian Forint, New Zealand Dollar, Norwegian Krone, Polish Zloty, Singapore Dollar, Swedish Krona, and Swiss Franc ... in fact, at one recent PayPal presentation a member of the audience was heard to say, "Who needs SEPA when you've got PayPal?"

♦ PayPal's international business represented 40% of all revenues in Q4 2006, up from 35% the year before.

In Europe, PayPal has 35 million customer accounts processing $8.4 billion of total payment volume in 2006 alone and, of those 35 million accounts, 15 million are in the UK, representing over a third of adults and half of all internet users.

PayPal's popularity is reflected in high penetration rates among online shoppers in the major European markets including the UK, Germany, France and Italy, with Forrester Research estimating that 23% of European online shoppers prefer paying with PayPal.

PayPal has also developed relationships with many leading European merchants, including Boots, DHL, Harrods, Meetic and Pixmania.

This leads us to the most interesting development within PayPal right now – PayPal Mobile.

PayPal Mobile

I have spent a long time expounding the fact that mobile telephones would become popular as a payments mechanism. Many have scoffed this idea over the years. For example, at a US tradeshow in November 2004 I was told by bankers that mobile payments were too insecure and it would be about a decade before they would take off, probably driven by a Wal-Mart or Virgin.

Well, it took about 15 months and it was PayPal which was in there first with PayPal Mobile.

PayPal Mobile was announced in February 2006, the first major such announcement in the USA, and was launched in the USA and Canada in April and the UK in June 2006.

The take-up has been pretty slow, but the first movements towards PayPal Mobile have been created by promotions such as "Text to buy Depeche Mode's Live CD of this Concert now". This was a PayPal promotion run at a Depeche Mode concert and, surprise surprise, nearly 10% of the audience texted the number to buy the CD.

(…)

How does it work?

PayPal Mobile's folks call it "physical hyperlinks". The idea is that you are on the train or walking down the high road and you see the poster for the latest Robbie Williams, Artic Monkeys or Lily Allen CD. The poster then has the line "Text to buy" on it, the PayPal Mobile logo and a code, such as RWRDJ for Robbie Williams track "Rock DJ". You then text the PayPal Mobile number with "RWRDJ" from your phone, get a call back to authenticate your transaction by entering your PIN and that's it. A bit like seeing 'click to buy' online as a hyperlink, the 'text to buy' is a physical hyperlink.

(…)

So why has PayPal Mobile not taken off big time?

Because it has very limited merchant uptake right now, and this is why those relationships with the merchants are key to PayPal Mobile's strategy, with a number of early markets kicking off the business such as music and charities.

Music is key for the reason stated above, as in you walk down the street, see the poster, get the music. It's instantaneous gratification and impulse purchasing with immediate satisfaction is a great way to shift digital goods.

(…)

The other focus of PayPal Mobile is charities. Why charities? Because you walk past the adverts for the charity today, and by the time you get home you have forgotten the website, the telephone number and the moment your heartstrings were being pulled to give. Now, with PayPal Mobile, you walk past the poster, see the cause and give.

Giving in real time, there and then.

That's why PayPal Mobile will work.

Why bankers don't get it

Now, if PayPal could see the future of mobile payments and bankers couldn't, wouldn't or didn't, then how come bankers didn't get into mobile first? I mean PayPal were the first major to launch a mobile payments service in the USA.

The reason is that traditional bankers generally don't get Pay-Pal because they live in the old world of payments – cash, card and cheque – whilst PayPal live in a new, brave world of social networking and person-to-person payments. All of this stuff is new to many bank decision-makers. Take a look at my earlier comment around mobile payments being a decade away from US banks in 2004.

In the same year, Heidi Miller, Head of the Treasury and Securities Services businesses at JPMorgan Chase, made these comments at SIBOS 2004:

> "Wouldn't you think that banks should be facilitating payments transactions for eBay? We have the customer relationships. We have the accounts. We have the clearing and settlement systems. In fact, PayPal transactions ride on the very same systems we banks have spent billions of dollars building. And yet the banks lost the deal, despite our natural advantages. In less than one year, PayPal built a person-to-person payments solution that met the needs of the market better than any built by banks in the past five years."

Ms. Miller is right. PayPal built a solution better than banks could build and made it work. And that is the vital difference because, you see, many banks trial and pilot new services ... but that's as far as it goes. They are not committed. They are just putting their toe in the water to see what it is and how it works, not trying to make it work. That's why it is a trial, a pilot ... a suck it and see.

Equally, many traditional bankers think that by the time it is working if they aren't the first to be there then they can always copy it because they trialled it. For example, one banker from a major European bank said to me in 2006:

> "The real reason PayPal works is the consumer's perception that they are safe. If I said, 'any time you buy something on the internet using our card, I will not allow you to be defrauded and will not hold you to account', do you think Pay-Pal would work?"

Yes! Of course, it would work. This guy thought that he could shut PayPal down just by giving a banker's guarantee for online payments. Mmmmm, now let's see, by giving a banker's guarantee you can eradicate this upstart with 133 million user accounts and 14 million merchants?

Too late, my friend.

In fact, the real insight into PayPal came from Geoff Iddison who heads up PayPal Europe. Geoff made an interesting comment at the Financial Services Club, which I chair, when he was talking about how PayPal started in Europe. At the time, he was looking for a bank partner to work with and took the PayPal European business plan around some of London's most prestigious banks to see if they would like to partner with him. Now, bear in mind that Geoff is ex-Sotheby's and Christie's ... in other words, he's an auctioneer, not a banker ... and he was quite surprised by how negative the banker's reactions were.

Many of them scoffed at the ambition of the plans and said that PayPal would probably achieve their three-year ambitions in about 10 years.

PayPal achieved them in nine months.

And Geoff made the comment: "if PayPal was run with a banker's mentality, PayPal would not exist today". He's right as well. After all, you don't meet many banking people in PayPal but visionaries, internet aficionados and folks who like being in a brave new world.

That's why bankers don't get PayPal or, to be more exact, why bankers have not worked out the brave new world.

(...)

PayPal's future

PayPal's future is bright and is strongly supported by the statistics. For example, a 2006 study by Booz Allen Hamilton estimates that debit and credit card issuers and acquirers will lose up to 30% of transactions to online retailers offering PayPal.

PayPal also have a driving vision and mission to be the global leader for online payments and to build the web's most convenient, secure, cost-effective payment solution respectively. This has now extended to mobile and, in the future, could just as easily head towards other payment services. For example, howsabout using PayPal in exchange for air miles, loyalty programs, even to exchange time units in complementary currencies?

I guess one day, you might even be using PayPal down at the local supermarket with a wave of your phone ... now there's a thought.

Happy 100-month birthday, PayPal.

Chapter 4 Remittances: where the money's at

The
**Complete
Banker**

Introduction

Remittances is a financial term for money transfer between people where one of them typically does not have a bank account. It's been best known as the business of the behemoth Western Union, who have built a multi billion dollar service out of getting money out of one country for delivery to another in a secure and effective manner. The business of remittances has recently been revolutionised by the massive uptick in migrant workers thanks to globalisation, along with mobile telecommunications. These changes are fundamentally challenging the traditional businesses of the money transfer companies, as well as more informal networks like Hawala. It will be interesting to see where it develops, as we are talking about a market worth over $300 billion a year.

Remittances and the need for financial inclusion (2010)

I chaired a dinner last night on remittances and it was pretty interesting. The term 'remittances' is generally used to refer to foreign workers sending money home and represents major GDP for many countries. For example, Tonga's remittances represent 40% of the country's GDP, Samoa's is 25%, Jamaica's is over 20% and the Philippines 10%. This is a big market, and a mature one.

Equally, it is not just about migrant workers as the appetite for transferring money internationally has extended far beyond itinerant workers to a vast and diverse cross-section of senders and receivers.

Some senders are using lo-tech systems like Hawala, whilst others are heavily linked via hi-tech mobiles ... meanwhile receivers are the same, with everyone assuming they receive through human interfaces and yet, if you study this area closely, more and more is being enabled via mobile.

For example, in the Philippines, SMART and Globe Telecom have been running riot in the remittances space for years:

◆ SMART is the leading mobile operator in the Philippines with over 25 million subscribers, and has been offering an SMS-based remittance service known as "SMART Padala" since 2004. This service allows expatriates to deposit money with partnering banks in areas where high concentrations of Filipinos live, such as Hong Kong, Yokohama, and Abu Dhabi, and to specify the SMART subscriber in the Philippines who is to receive the money. The service sends a text message to both the sender and the recipient, notifying them that the money has been transferred. The recipient can then use his/her mobile account to specify the desired withdrawal amount and pick it up at a partnering institution in the Philippines.

◆ The Philippines' second mobile operator, Globe Telecom, offers a similar service known as G-Cash. At participating remittance companies in the US, the UK, Australia, and Taiwan, Filipino workers can send money via an SMS message to Globe subscribers in the Philippines. The recipient can pick up the cash from any Globe Telecom store by showing his mobile phone (with the SMS message) and a form of personal identification.

And if you wonder whether low-income folks want mobile money, then this is the place to look. For example, a study by the microfinance and remittance focused organisation CGAP found that targeting low income users could succeed.

"Philippines is known as the texting capital of the world but we were working in provinces that were poorer and where literacy levels were lower than the national norm. What we found is true in most markets globally: younger people whose social lives involve being connected via cell phones

Money for Nothing and your Cheques for Free

and people with exposure to using computers are more comfortable using cell phones to begin with."

The result is that 80% of money movements in the Philippines is now made electronically. A decade ago, 80% would have been physical movements of cash. That's transformational and is why one of the folks at the table said that: "if you don't know what is happening with technology these days, then you've lost the plot".

This increase in access to electronic and formal channels for money transfer, rather than physical and informal channels, is rapidly changing the dynamics of connectivity and funding.

For example, microfinance is now becoming a major focal point, as is financial inclusion, and it amazed me that everyone talked about mobile for money transfer during our discussion but no-one talked about social networks. And when I did raise the subject of Kiva as a social lending microfinance service, one of the bankers asked me: "what's Kiva?" Surely, being in this space, banks should know about these developments?

Another said the lack of commentary on social media and microfinance was more of a reflection of the fact that young people use social networks and the average age of a remittance sender and receiver is around 37.

I then added that the average age of a Facebook user is 42 and Twitter users are generally over 35s.

Silence.

If you don't know what is happening with technology these days, then you've lost the plot.

The nature of networks, mobile internet and social finance is changing all of our lives fundamentally and is as true in the remittances space as any other. Ignoring such fundamental changes is likely to leave the existing money transfer firms dead in the wake of dynamic societal change.

For example, the likelihood of a divide between informal networks using human carriers of money versus formal networks using mobile internet is the clear path of the future. This inevitably raises critical questions for existing providers of Money Transfer such as Western Union, Travelex and the banks.

And these are the themes we explored in depth last night.

It was interesting that one theme that kept cropping up regularly was 'trust'. I always hear trust in the context of banking and payments, so challenged what it is that is trusted.

For example, the Philippine GCASH Service is delivered in partnership with financial institutions and banks. Why? Because, according to the banks, customers trust the service if a bank is involved. Sure. They trust the service, not because they trust the bank but because they trust the banking infrastructure to guarantee movement of funds.

So the trust is in the system, not the individual bank or financial partner involved.

That's one critical point.

Another is that this market – especially if we talk more about financial inclusion – involves so many players. It cannot be led by a bank or mobile operator, but needs to be led by a collaborative effort of banks, mobile carriers, government agencies, regulators and more. It may even need involvement of security services and police, as half the dialogue about money transfer is focused upon terrorism. "9/11 was funded by hundreds of sub-$1,000 transactions through the money transfer markets", was one of the comments made last night. Sure, but is the role of a money transfer service to allow simplicity of money transfer or to monitor the pulse of terrorism?

I would argue that it is both, which is why so many organisations need a hand in these markets: global regulatory authorities, national governments, police and security forces, banks and infrastructure providers, mobile and electronic service organisations, software and technology firms ... and money transfer agents, of course.

This led to an interesting debate at the end of the evening about the role of banks in money transfer markets and their interest, or lack of interest, in remittances.One banker said that: "any dramatic change in the past will not have been noticed by the bank and any dramatic change in the future will not be noticed because these changes happen locally, not globally".

Another reckoned it was because banks are not able to make money out of money transfers, but can lose money: "on a $1,000 transaction, we make about $10 if we're lucky but, if you mess up, the costs are anything up to $100 million in fines and over $1 billion in lost business due to reputational damage."

I disagreed with that view as, if banks felt that way, you wouldn't be performing any payments processing for anyone. In fact, a point came up that surely this was a corporate and social responsibility and that if banks are not interested in remittances today, and the market continues to grow, then at what point will banks start to wonder why they are disintermediated from these markets and wish they had been involved?

We concluded that, in order for remittances to really rock and roll in the future, it needed three things:

1   **A goal:** there must be some collaborative objective and mission to be reached;

2   **A reason:** there needs to be some skin in the game and value returned for all players; and

3   **A cause:** there needs to be a common enemy to cause the players to do this, such as the threat of regulatory change.

With the above, then a multi-industry group could potentially be created to burst the bubble of financial exclusion and move us to a completely connected global society of commerce.

More on remittances (2010)

I mentioned a dinner which I chaired about remittances the other day, and the firm that organised the dinner sent me a white paper as a follow-up.

This is a summary of the paper.

"Remittances are no longer solely about supporting people in the developing world. in many cases today, remittances are also made for charitable and trade reasons and can therefore have a very powerful impact, especially if directed for maximum benefit. findings of a recent World Bank report indicate that the rate of return to each dollar of aid directed toward promoting trade is nearly $700 in additional trade.

"This discussion covered pertinent industry issues including how the global uptake of mobile, internet and social network communications is dramatically changing the landscape.

"Interestingly, participants' perspectives also suggested that, in spite of technology being more affordable and accessible, the old world of payments – face-to-face contact and cash-based transaction – continues to command a foothold, albeit a weaker one.

"The debate turned to the roles that financial institutions and regulatory bodies are currently playing, as well as their future potential impact. this led to dialogue about the ongoing problem of the unbanked and financial exclusion in the latter part of the discussion.

"Participants offered some sound suggestions of how this can be tackled, including how transferred monies can be used for trade reform."

Why banks should avoid the remittance market (2010)

Great conversations continue in the remittances space, or money transfer space if you prefer, with a chat with the global transaction services folks from a major bank.

This bank has a dilemma: are they in the remittances space or are they not? They really want to be in this space but are worried about risk exposures, particularly reputational risk.

Their challenge is to find out whether there's enough profit in remittances to be worth the risk. They recognise that processing money transfers is a good business to be in. It can make money for them, and would fill in some missing pieces of their transaction services business.

Not just that, but it may be critical for them. For example, they see mobile money transfer as being key to their future, and see the use of mobile and transaction services as being so obvious that it's a no brainer for them to be in this space.

They would like to do this in partnership with one of the major mobile carriers as, if they aren't in partnership, others will be and that is dangerous as there are only so many partners out there. If Deutsche Bank gets T-Mobile for example, and Citi gets AT&T, HSBC gets Hutchinson, Bank of Tokyo-Mitsubishi gets KDDI and Royal Bank of Scotland gets Vodafone, then there aren't that many mobile firms left to partner with. Soon, the markets are stitched up and banks that want to be mobile payments processors globally will be left in the cold.

Hmmmm.

Meanwhile, the real dilemma is why would a mobile carrier want to be the partner?

Sure, it's not their business to process payments although, as they are also transaction processors, they can find this extension of their core business something they could implement quite easily.

Mobile carriers are also used to dealing with small account-holders. Think of your son or daughter's mobile account. How much is spent per month and how many transactions are made? Maybe a few hundred text messages and a few telephone calls? Maybe €5 to €10 of cost per month. That's diddly-squat, so mobile carriers are used to processing high volume, low margin transactions on masse.

And what's the real game changer for mobile? Reach.

Every person on the planet can probably get access to a mobile handset if they wanted – there are over four billion users out there – and so mobile carriers want to enable financial transactions for all of their customers.

And there's the rub: a bank only wants to deal with profitable customers, which is why only a billion people on the planet are banked, whilst carriers want to work with all customers, and three out of four are unbanked.

Now that wouldn't be an issue: a bank could offer remittance and money transfers for the three out of four who are unbanked, but it is a problem because banks need to comply with AML and KYC rules. Mobile carriers don't provide that information and, in many instance, they don't get or need that information. Mobiles can be picked up and SIM cards used anonymously.

That's no good for a bank ... although if the account is only €5 a month, maybe that is OK as banks do support limited use pre-paid cards anonymously. But then mobiles are topped up and that additional value needs to be monitored.

So, you now have mobile carriers starting to come in to the AML and KYC rules.

For example, on e African money transfer operator told me that customers are being instructed to re-register their telephones with some form of identification in some countries.

All well and good you may say, but then a banker replied that that is OK except that the mobile firms just get an ID with no proof of correct details. For the banks, they need all the customer's details plus proof to ensure the correct ID is being presented via utility bills and other means.

So there is an issue here. But let's say that it is solvable.

Then there's still another issue: profit.

For a bank, the risk versus reward equation for remittances is skewed heavily against the money transfer market. For example, several banks got into buying money transfer operations during the first half of the last decade as global migrant worker movements exploded. They thought they could cross-sell to the users of these services and, as migrants became more affluent, maybe get them fully banked along with their family.

But this was not the case.

For example, Spanish banks tell me that the users they thought they could cross-sell to in Spain already had bank accounts. They just used the remittance service because it was cheaper, faster and more reliable than using the bank.

Hence, the cross-sell dream was a flawed vision. And there are hardly any profits in remittances unless you're a really big player with massive volume. In fact, on that note, it's getting worse as the credit crisis means that not only are there fewer migrant workers these days, as many have moved back home, but the ones that remain are sending less money home. So margins are tight, there's no growth in volumes or values, and profits are almost non-existent.

But let's say you overcome the issue of AML and profitability, then what? There's another issue: coverage.

To be a player in this game, you need a lot of agents – Moneygram has 200,000 agents worldwide, for example – to disburse payments and manage accounts. Those agents need appropriate licensing and vetting, and that's a challenge for a bank. Even if you have all the agents, you then need geographic coverage – Money-gram has reach to over 160 countries – and most banks do not have that coverage and, in the case of some, don't want it.

For example, think about an American bank. An American bank would have no issue covering global service provision ... except when you start talking about coverage in Iran maybe. Or in Pakistan and other politically sensitive country operations.

Now these banks start to worry that they might have an exposure like the one that UBS encountered. When the American forces broke open Saddam Hussein's vaults in Baghdad, they found millions of dollars of crisp new dollar bills. However, the US had outlawed the supply of US dollars to Iraq for over a decade, so how did they get there? The Fed investigated and found the currencies came through other outlawed nations including Libya and Syria, via branches of UBS. Result: UBS was fined $100 million which, at the time, was one of the largest fines ever made for a bank infringement of US regulations.

So there's the rub. Even if you can organise money transfers, monitor things well, get the AML and KYC in place and operate profitability, a bank still has a huge reputational risk exposure if they get heavily into the remittances market.

Let's say you can overcome all of this though, as a bank, then what?

Well, there's a final issue: smell.

Banks think migrant workers are smelly and don't want them in their branches and migrant workers think that banks are smelly, as they look down their noses at them.

You may think it over-states that case, but one French bank openly stated that they did not want to be in remittance services because they don't want these "poor, foreign workers" in their branches.

And these "poor, foreign workers" often feel intimidated by bank lobbies and branches, and the sort of people who use them,

Money for Nothing and your Cheques for Free

so would rather deal with someone who speaks their language who they feel they can trust more.

There are loads of other points that could be made here but, all in all, even if you can organise money transfers, deal with the AML and KYC issues, find a way to make some money and manage the high reputational risk, a bank shouldn't be getting into remittances because it does not smell right.

So who will make this space their own?

Hmmm ... now who are leading the remittances and financial inclusion space today?

Oh yes, Safaricom/Vodafone (M-PESA) and a few other mobile carriers and operators.

And so the real dilemma is: why would a mobile carrier want to be the partner?

Now it gets interesting...

Escape with Phones4U (2009)

Just got a really interesting note about a new MasterCard from Phones4U. It's called the 'Escape' Card and focuses upon migrant worker remittances.

What's interesting is that it has been launched by the mobile phone shop Phones4U, a completely non-bank non-carrier operation that is just a pure retailer of mobile telephony.
Here's the shortened write-up:

> "The new Escape MasterCard Prepaid Card will change the way people get money to friends and family abroad.
>
> It's the cheapest way; in fact it's completely free.
>
> It's one of the cheapest pay-as-you-go cards around because there are no usage and monthly fees plus it's free to load with cash at Phones 4u (a UK mobile phone shop) ...
>
> In 2007, a whopping £3.1 billion left the UK* for friends and family abroad.

Money saved in fees could mean that you are able to add more to the amount your family or friends receive.

The card will save time and money for the 400,000** people who regularly move money abroad to family and friends.

As well as no surplus charges, it can be done over phone, text or the internet 24 hours a day and it only takes 60 seconds for the money to reach the other side (of the world). Compared to the usual 48 hours and £20+ it can take with the Western Union, that's a lot of time and money saved.

Ethnic minority groups are twice as likely to live on a low income*** which means the benefits of banking facilities aren't always an option.

*source: Developing Market Associates, 2007
**source: BME Remittance Survey 2006
***source: Joseph Rowntree Foundation, 2008"

This proves interesting because we all know that remittances is a key market ripe for the picking ... and what is the most likely place a migrant worker will visit when settling in a new country?

The mobile phone shop. And just in case the migrant worker hasn't worked that fact out, they even created a little video to explain how to open the card account.

Yowsa!

More on remittances (2009)

After my previous discussions on remittances, it is timely to talk about this as it relates to the G8 Summit taking place in Italy this week.

During the build-up to this meeting campaigners have been reminding the leaders of their obligations to Africa, especially Italy and France who reneged on their pledges of 2005. Bob

Geldof wasn't going to let them get away with that, and publicly shamed Silvio Berlusconi into an apology.

With this in mind, a key part of the G8 meeting will focus upon remittances, as this payments process has a critical role to play in the health and wealth of Africa. For example, a few choice snippets from recent news includes:

> "The collapse of international capital markets and the recession in major economies have halved growth in Sub-Saharan Africa. Combined with falling national income from commodity prices and remittances, and the increasing cost of food and energy, this will seriously retard progress towards the Millennium Development Goals (MDGs), pushing tens of millions more Africans below the poverty line."

(Sean Leno, CBC Africa Forum)

> "The world's poorest countries will see $1tn (£600bn) drain from their economies this year according to the first detailed analysis of how the global recession is hitting developing nations."

(The *Guardian*, June 2009)

> "One area that holds promise pertains to remittances by the African Diaspora. Remittances have become a major source of financing for Africa's development, and in some countries, they are more important than aid. Remittances are however sensitive to economic conditions and the recent crisis has resulted in significant reductions of remittances to Africa."

(Brookings Institute, July 2009)

> "Poor people are being forced to shoulder multiple burdens that are not of their making. The economic crisis is hitting their remittances and investment and trade flows. Climate change is harming their harvests, livelihoods, health and

4 : Remittances: where the money's at

safety. High food and commodity prices are worsening a chronic poverty crisis which continues to claim thousands of lives every day. You can make health care and education a reality for millions of people if you keep your promise to pay $50 billion in foreign aid."

(Letter from Annie Lennox, Colin Firth, Scarlett Johansson, Angélique Kidjo, Bill Nighy and many others to the G8)

What this train of thought clearly shows is that the financial markets and financial providers have a key role to play in the health of nations through the wealth of nations.

A remittance strategy scribble (2009)

Remittances continually intrigues me as a market, especially the major focus financial institutions are now placing on this area as an opportunity. This is contradictory as those who need remittance services the most are often those who do not use banks or have bank accounts. So there's an anomaly there. Nevertheless, the banks' interests are probably something to do with the fact that there's $375 billion worth of remittances sent around the world every year.

First, we need to consider exactly what a remittance is.

Most folks think of a remittance as money transfer from a migrant worker to their family in another country, with 14 major sending countries to 72 receiving countries according to the World Bank.

These are:

◆ Canada to India; Vietnam; Jamaica; Haiti;

◆ France to Senegal; Mali; Côte d'Ivoire; Haiti; Morocco; Tunisia; India; Vietnam; China; Algeria;

- Germany to Turkey; Lebanon; Serbia; India; Romania; Bosnia and Herzegovina; Croatia; Morocco; China;

- Italy to India; Philippines; Albania; Romania; Serbia; Nigeria; Sri Lanka; Morocco; China;

- Japan to Philippines; China; Korea; Brazil; Peru;

- Malaysia to Indonesia;

- Netherlands to Morocco; Suriname; Nigeria; Turkey; Indonesia; Netherlands Antilles; Ghana; Dominican Republic;

- Russia to Armenia; Kyrgyz Republic; Belarus; Moldova; Azerbaijan; Georgia; Ukraine; Tajikistan; Kazakhstan; Uzbekistan; Latvia; Lithuania; Estonia;

- Saudi Arabia to Pakistan; Yemen; Bangladesh; India; Philippines; Egypt; Jordan;

- Singapore to Bangladesh; India; Malaysia; China; Indonesia; Pakistan

- South Africa to Swaziland; Lesotho; Zimbabwe; Angola; Botswana; Mozambique; Malawi; Zambia;

- Spain to Dominican Republic; Colombia; Peru; Brazil; Romania; Ecuador; Philippines; Morocco; Bulgaria; China;

- United Kingdom to Brazil; Pakistan; Poland; Bangladesh; Nepal; Sri Lanka; Philippines; India; Sierra Leone; Nigeria; Ghana; Lithuania; Uganda; Romania; Bulgaria; South Africa; Jamaica; Kenya; Albania; Zambia; Rwanda; China;

- United States to Ecuador; Vietnam; El Salvador; Peru; India; Nigeria; Ghana; Guatemala; Honduras; Colombia; Jamaica; Mexico; Philippines; Haiti; Dominican

Republic; Guyana; Indonesia; Brazil; Pakistan; China; Lebanon; Thailand.

The primary receiving countries are India (15% of global remittances), Mexico, Philippines, China (8% each), Turkey (6%) and Egypt (5%), and the top 16 receiving countries represent 75% of all remittance receipts.

All of this is fluid however, as economic migration is predicated on economic health and, as seen recently in the UAE, if the economies falter then so does the economic migration:

It's the great escape by Indians who've hit the dead-end in Dubai. Local police have found at least 3,000 automobiles – sedans, SUVs, regulars – abandoned outside Dubai International Airport in the last four months.

Nevertheless, global remittances is big business, particularly as the traditional model of money transfer – via an agent's office such as Western Union's or via Hawala – is changing thanks to technology.

With half the world now able to access mobile telephones, the remittances space is being re-engineered. This was illustrated well by the rise of m-Pesa in Kenya – from nothing to 7 million subscribers in just two years making this the largest financial services in the country – which led to the announcement by Citibank of an agreement with Vodafone to emulate the success of the service worldwide.

Since then, Vodafone have linked with other providers, such as Western Union, and mobile and prepaid remittances are definitely worthy of note.

This led to an illumination for me last week, which is that it is not the transfer of money or the technology which drives this marketplace ... it is how to get value from person to person. Whether the transfer of value is via an agent, mobile telephone, card or other service does not matter. Purely the accessibility to sending value and receiving value.

Money for Nothing and your Cheques for Free

In this context, the sender typically lives in a developed or growing economy – France, Germany, Italy, Spain UK, Russia, Saudi Arabia, South Africa, Japan, Singapore, Malaysia, USA, Canada – to one that is underbanked and often underdeveloped.

In other words, from countries with high density of technology access to countries with lower or poor access to technology.

With this in mind, I felt a chart for a remittance strategy could look something like:

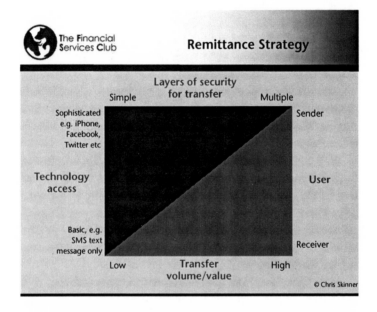

In other words, this aims to provide sender's with sophisticated and ubiquitous access points to send value via any technology channel, including anything from an iPhone app to a money transfer agency ... through to receiver's being offered simple and ubiquitous access via the most appropriate channels for the culture and country infrastructure which for many will be SMS text messages and / or a money transfer agency.

Oh yes, and value could be monetary remittances, but it doesn't have to be. It might be airmiles, loyalty points for telephone or food services, or even games, ringtones and anything else that has a value ...

This is just a scribble on the back of a notepad at this stage, but may be worth fleshing out into something more substantial.

Remittances numbers (2009)

I've often talked about the remittance markets and chaired a meeting today where SWIFT, Wells Fargo, Earthport, Citi, Western Union, ICICI Bank and more outlined the progress in this area.

The following stats give the state of the nation:

◆ There are around $375 billion of remittances sent around the world every year, up from $300 billion last year;

◆ Almost half of all remittances are sent through informal networks, including friends, family and non-electronic means such as Hawala;

◆ Banks have less than a quarter of the global remittance market movements of funds due to a lack of standards such as IBAN and BIC for account details, a lack of connectivity between bank systems cross-borders and a general opaqueness of charging structures and FX costs;

◆ This may be resolved through the SWIFT initiative to provide standards, where a pilot system has been running for a few months with 27 banks onboard, with plans for a full launch in April 2009;

◆ The main sending countries are the USA, Russia, Saudi and various European countries;

Money for Nothing and your Cheques for Free

- The main receiving countries are India, China, Mexico and the Philippines;

- India is the largest receiving country for remittances, with $50 billion flowing inwards annually: 40% from the USA, 40% from the Gulf Cooperation Council (GCC) countries, 14% from Europe and only 6% from South-East Asia;

- In China, there are 25 million migrant workers according to official figures, although this is estimated to be up to 100 million workers unofficially;

- The Philippines receives around $16 billion of remittances each year, and this has been growing by over 20% year-on-year;

- The GCC accounts for much of the growth globally, but expect a 9% downturn this year due to shrinkage in the global economies;

- Although growth is slowing due to the global downturn in markets, there is still double-digit growth in remittances as workers are still 'migrating';

- The average cost of a US$200 transfer across borders involves fees and FX charges of 9.96% compared to only 6.21% on a remittance of US$500;

- The turnover for the remittance market is estimated to be $400 billion globally by 2011 and yet only 1% of this is forecast to be made via mobile transfers due to a lack of standards and co-ordinated response;

- The average time that Xoom measured for a remittance payment to move to a receiver's account after leaving the clearing system from the sender's account is 56 hours; and

◆ Due to increased competition and customer demand, banks are moving to faster forms of remittance payment from immediate to same day to non-urgent, and customers are happy to pay higher prices for the certainty of immediate and same day payments.

Chapter 5 Regulation: from SEPA to PSD, and beyond

The
**Complete
Banker**

Introduction

In Europe, there has been a massive change programme to create a harmonised payments area where all euro payments are treated as though they are domestic payments. That's a tough call, as there are 16 countries in the Eurozone in 2010, and for all of their banks to process payments across those countries as though they are domestic is a tough call. That's why the banks created SEPA – the Single Euro Payments Area – supported by new European regulation to ensure it's all kosher, the PSD – the Payment Services Directive. Funnily enough, just as all of this went live in November 2009, the Eurozone almost collapsed. Oh, the strange games we play.

What happens to SEPA, Chi-X etc if the euro fails? (2010)

There's the classic old joke about the European dream being a place where the police are English, the chefs are Italian, the car mechanics are German, the lovers are French and the bankers are all Swiss. The nightmare is that it is a place where the police are German, the chefs are English, the car mechanics are French, the lovers are Swiss and the bankers are Italians.

It seems that the nightmare is coming true, although the basket case is Greece and the bankers are German.

Last week's surprising comments from German Chancellor Angela Merkel that "the euro is in danger" and "if the euro fails, Europe fails" sent shudders across the world's markets, and probably made Brussels shake with rage.

But the Germans are shaking with rage. After Nicolas Sarkozy was rumoured to threaten Merkel with France's withdrawal from the euro if she didn't step up to the plate and support a Greek bailout, Germany's citizens have been demonstrating their rage by printing Deutschemarks whilst the national newspaper, *Bild*, is stirring anger towards the EU and the Greeks in particular with headlines such as:

- "How much more do we have to pump into this country?" April 26th

- "Why are we paying the luxury pensions of the Greeks?" April 27th

- "Greeks ready to cut back? They would rather strike!" April 28th

As I talk to German colleagues, they refer to Greece as the Golden Fleece and that they aren't paying bills in Greek restaurants because they've prepaid to 2020.

All of this puts a huge strain on the European Union, in its fragile 53rd year of unity, particularly as Spain, Italy and Portugal are considered to be on a par with Greece by many, forming a Southern European Union called the PIGS (Portugal, Italy, Greece and Spain).

It raises a key question in my mind, and I'm sure all of the bankers I deal with: if the euro fails, what happens to the monetary union of banks, the Financial Services Action Plan and all those bank and insurance directives like Solvency II, MiFID and the PSD?

What happens to Chi-X, SEPA, the EBA and the rest?

In order to answer this question, you have to look at two key areas. First, is the economic and monetary union (EMU) broken? Second, if it is, do we throw away the 18 years of change introduced by the agreement to launch the euro when the Maastricht Treaty was signed in February 1992?

Let's take the first question: is the EMU broken?

We asked this question in 2005, when the French and Dutch threw out the EU Treaty. Answer: it is political union that they were rejecting, not economic union. Note: even with their rejection, and the Irish no vote, the Treaty became the Lisbon

Money for Nothing and your Cheques for Free

Treaty in 2010 regardless of such resistance. In other words, in the interests of the long-term vision of Europe, Europe wins.

Equally, America has taken years to gain its 'United' status, starting with a nation of disparate states that had far less history than those of Europe. Their Union was easier in comparison, and that still took years, so Europe's union will take time and will face many more tests.

But this is the greatest test so far.

The size of this test should not be underestimated as it is the first time that we are seeing an economic union, resulting in a cascading effect upon money and politics. Historically, the tests for Europe have been mainly about how much power is ceded to Brussels. This test is showing the inter-relationship between economies and Germany's anguish is that if they are to keep the vision of Europe in harmony, then they have to pay for it.

Therefore, returning to the rejection of the European constitution, that was a political rejection and when a country has an economic crisis, the monetary union means that other nations pay and, as a result, that political will is tested when one nation's tax dollars are taken to pay for another nation's debts.

That is why this challenge is so much greater than any before, because it is testing the political will of citizens, not just their ability to trade and compete.

The core issue though, is that it is not just the Greek economy and Greece that would leave the Union if they were allowed to fail. It is the Union.

Should the Greek economy fail to honour their government bonds due to being economically bankrupt, the ratings agencies and banks would downgrade Spain, Portugal and Italy, and there would be a spiral effect. This means the European Union breaks apart.

That is why the Greek failure option is unpalatable ... but is the alternative palatable?

Why do we need a European Union?

Answer: Europe needs to be a Union to maintain its drive to be a regional superpower, and competitive commercially and economically with China and America. There's the rub. If Europe fails, then the UK, Germany and France fail, as parity to compete internationally and intra-region becomes far more difficult.

This is why Greece needs the bailout and why Germans are paying.

It does not help Angela Merkel maintain her status or power hold in Germany – her popularity is sinking faster than the Titanic – but if Greece fails, it is felt that Europe may fail too. And that is not an option seen to be agreeable today.

Also, nations have been bailed out already.

Two years ago, Spanish banks received over €50 billion worth of 'aid', in the form of mortgage-backed securities with the European Central Bank (ECB), when they faced a property meltdown.

Did the Germans wail out about that bailout? No. Why? Because it wasn't on the front page of the *Bild*. That bailout was smaller and less obvious, so no-one really noticed.

The Greek bailout is a bit bigger – €110 billion – admittedly, but it is supported by the IMF and is necessary for Europe's future. Enough said, although if you want to know more, Robert J Samuelson in the *Washington Post* provides a particularly good overview of why Europe needs to support Greece.

My summation is that Europe will survive this crisis, the euro will stay and the currently ridiculous pricing of US$1.24 to the euro will reverse within the next month or so, as forecasted by most economists.

Money for Nothing and your Cheques for Free

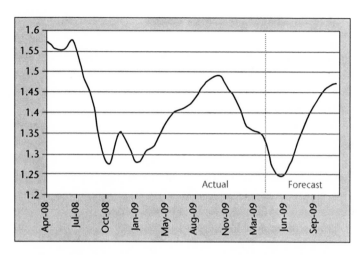

But let's look at the worst case scenario: what do we do if the euro does fail? Does it mean we unravel all we've done to date?

This is the second and, in some ways, more important question: is there a backup plan?

OK, if the Eurozone breaks apart, then it matters ... but it will not throw away all that has been built to date. The banks will still want to use cross-border instruments that work. They will just bring back a margin to represent those cross-border movements whilst maintaining the efficiency of the infrastructure that has been built.

As Werner Steinmuller, Head of Global Transaction Services of Deutsche Bank, stated when we researched the Payment Services Directive (PSD) and the Single Euro Payments Area (SEPA) last year:

> "Deutsche Bank is in a comfortable situation. We spent quite a sizeable amount on SEPA infrastructure and have a brand new system that is extremely capable of doing this that is also highly scalable. Others have not made this investment so this gives us a price advantage. We have built some conversion so-

lutions for handling old volumes and now can run both old instruments and the new SEPA instruments so, if SEPA is coming, we are extremely well positioned. If SEPA fails, I can write off the investments and still win."

In other words, the SEPA process has forced the banks to build new infrastructure, new systems and new efficiencies in transaction processing. That will stay. It does not go away if the euro goes away, as the new infrastructure is designed to handle efficient transactions, not euro payments.

So if we look at SEPA Credit Transfers and Direct Debits, the Euro Banking Association (EBA) and STEP2 ... it will all stay. The EBA will be a private consortium to operate efficient systems, rather than a government initiative to create efficiency, and it will stay. There will be a charge for this, and a charge that could provide a substantial return to the banks that created this infrastructure, but it will not go away.

The same will be true for Chi-X, and the capabilities electronic trading platforms have introduced into the European equities markets. Sure, some countries may want to block and reverse policies in these areas – Spain? – but the process of regional investing is unstoppable now. Goldmans, Merrill, BarCap and co, won't want to see this go away, so it will remain.

Bottom line: the efficiency of European payments and investing is in the interest of banks, corporates and institutions today, not just governments and policymakers.

So, if the euro fails, my answer is that the all the investment made by the financial markets in efficient systems will stay.

It will just be at a profit rather than a regulation.

A new PSD-approved Payments Institution starts business (2010)

Nick Ogden, CEO and founder of Voice Commerce (he previously created WorldPay, the RBS payments unit, back in 1993 and sold it to them in 2002*), recently spoke at the Financial Services Club about using voice biometrics as part of authentication in mobile financial transactions.

Who is Voice Commerce Group? Best to read what they say about themselves:

> "The Voice Commerce Group was founded upon a simple principle 'whenever we speak we establish a position of trust'. Consumers use their voices to communicate decisions; perhaps to instruct, to agree or to buy something. This natural process already happens automatically billions of times every day and the Voice Commerce Group has taken this natural capability and automated the process through its innovation in voice signatures.

> "Voice signatures allow consumers to use their own unique voice to sign and authorise transactions, and their patented technology now lies behind worldwide standards for mobile trust. Using voice signatures guarantees transactional security when making a payment and protects users against personal data compromise. Voice signatures are complex devices that combine the use of voice biometrics with transactional history, trends and patterns to create a highly secure, unique authorisation environment. The system can deliver two factor identity authentications virtually anywhere. Authorisation failures, suspected imposters or potential fraudsters can be controlled and managed and transactions re-qualified using automated outbound IVR. This not only improves customer service but reduces the risk of fraud and identity theft."

Why am I giving them a plug here?

Because, during the evening at the FSClub, Nick mentioned that Voice Commerce were one of the first Payments Institutions (PI) to register with the FSA, after the PSD was transposed last November and were about to announce that they are also one of the first PIs to be accepted as a Principal Member of Visa Europe.

The announcement was released this morning, so now is the time to talk about it.

What does being a Principal Member of Visa Europe mean? The membership means Voice Commerce can start providing its own payment services to businesses including acquiring payment transactions.

Following the launch of the PSD in November 2009, Visa Europe confirmed that Payment Service Providers such as Voice Commerce, as defined in the PSD, would be eligible to apply to become members of Visa Europe. Subject to stringent risk management requirements and being capable of complying with Visa Europe's operating regulations, the Voice Commerce application was approved by Visa Europe at the Board of Directors Meeting in February 2010.

Nick comments that:

> "as a Payment Institution, Voice Commerce is regulated in exactly the same way as banks in relation to capital adequacy and regulatory responsibilities for payment services. Being granted Visa membership means we can further compete on an equal footing across Europe with our banking peers. Our next move will be to grow the business and bring fresh creativity to the industry using innovative payment services, including voice biometrics to authorise payments."

Voice Commerce also describe themselves as being "athorised by (the) UK Financial services Authority under the European Commission Payment Service Directive, and regulated

115

in the provision of e-money services". This means that they have to "maintain appropriate financial capital adequacy".

Interesting. Very interesting. Particularly interesting as the firm that Nick created, WorldPay, is now up for sale with a price tag of £3 billion ($4.5 billion).

Bidders include private equity firms Advent International Corp; TPG Inc.; Warburg Pincus LLC; Kohlberg, Kravis Roberts & Co; Permira; CVC Capital Partners, Blackstone Group LLP and The Carlyle Group LLP. Tsys, Atos, ChasePaymentTech and First Data are rumoured to be in there ... and IT firm Voice Commerce Group, whose chairman and chief executive officer is Nick Ogden, the founder of Worldpay, is making a bid to get them back too!

From Lafferty Card News:

> "A skilled management team has already been assembled as part of the acquisition offer that will include the existing team at Voice Commerce. The team has appointed Montrose Partners, specialist financial advisors, to assist in their bid ... the value of Ogden's bid for RBS WorldPay has still to decided, but he said Voice Commerce has substantial support from a number of private equity firms. When asked when a deal might be completed, he said: 'The expectation from UBS, who are handling the deal, is hopefully by August 2010. The process of due diligence is now taking place while they attain the position and value of the company. Following this period, UBS are expected to produce a sales memorandum in January 2010. Voice Commerce then predicts an 18-month separation process of the business, at which point the full extent of the deal will become clear.'"

This house believes that SEPA does matter ... or does it? (2010)

We had a great debate at the Financial Services Club the other day, with the provocative title:

> "This house believes that SEPA (the Single Euro Payments Area) does matter".

The evening was chaired by the more than capable Bob Lyddon, who coordinates the IBOS Association secretariat, and four panel members who 'played' parts in being proposes and opposer of the motion. Proposing the motion were two leading European Proponents: Gilbert Lichter, CEO of the Euro Banking Association (EBA) Clearing Company that runs STEP2, a Pan-European ACH; and Fred Bär, Managing Director for Euro Services at Vocalink. Opposing the motion were two devilish Brits, set up in the form of Paul Smee, Chief Executive of the UK Payments Council and Simon Bailey of Logica.

On the night, Bob kicked off the motion by making clear that there are four immutable facts about SEPA which were not up for debate. These are that there is no end-date set as of today (although I think one is coming); the Core and B2B SEPA Direct Debits schemes are in production; the fact that there is no requirement for central bank reporting for transactions under €50,000 is good for efficiency; and cross-border direct debit and credit transfer euro transactions must now cost the same as domestic transactions.

With those four foundation points, Bob then asked Gilbert to take the floor.

Gilbert gave a resoundingly balanced view, stating that the old days of cross-border margins and operations were a luxury. The way correspondent banks worked and the form filling required for cross-border payments were a big issue in inhibiting trade across Europe, and those days are now gone as European

Commission Regulation 924/2009 makes it clear that every bank in Europe must now be reachable for SEPA Direct Debits.

As these changes will alter the behaviours of payments processors and payments users, innovations will follow, as innovation follows buying behaviours. By way of example, Gilbert cited Spain where SEPA payments have increased from 3.5% of transactions to 13.6% in the last quarter.

All of this means that SEPA does matter, because it is fundamentally changing European commerce and pushes banks to the management table.

Paul Smee responded with a worrying opening line that SEPA reminded him of the old Samuel Johnson saying that 'a woman's preaching is like a dog's walking on his hind legs. It is not done well; but you are surprised to find it done at all'.

Paul's comment was far more relevant to SEPA than the incorrectness of the statement however, in that if SEPA were that needed, then how come there haven't been any SEPA street parties yet to celebrate. Again, I would claim that there have been a few ... but then SIBOS, EBA Days and IPS aren't exactly street parties are they, as we all celebrate inside bars of the world, but there you go.

Paul continued by saying that the reason for the lack of celebrations is down to the fact that:

- ◆ SEPA is not critical and nor are payments. No-one wakes up thinking about how important any of this is, unless you abolish cheques;

- ◆ SEPA doesn't matter because it has been a top-down process driven by politicians with no user involvement. The European Payments Council (EPC) must engage with the user communities, such as those represented by the UK Payments Council, for this to succeed; and SEPA is not working because, based upon the UK's experience with the Faster Payments Service, if you have a regulatory mandate involving technology change, IT will support this but the business community will not. In other words, SEPA needs a business requirement to succeed, not just a technology change.

A few heckles raised meant that it was time for the seconder of the motion, Fred Bär, to respond to Paul's comments.

Fred began with comments that banks do innovate, with the direct debit being a good example, but it can take a long time to be pervasive especially when there are so many constituencies, groups and actors involved (was he referring to Simon?). That is why it will take 20 years for a baby of this size to be born. Never-the-less, the fact that it is so difficult – with IBAN and BIC usage being a good case in point – does not make it worthless and SEPA is worthwhile and does matter.

However, it could have mattered more if the launch of the infrastructure was supported by a regulation that mattered. Unfortunately, this regulation – the Payments Services Direc-tive – lost all credibility just as things were moving forward, and when we were at a point when the regulation needed to be more credible than ever before.

Then the Phantom that is Simon stood up and delivered the most damning attack on the program of all of the evening's speak-ers who, remember, are all playing 'a part' in the program and do not necessarily believe the views they are presenting.

Anyways, Simon began by asking what exactly is SEPA, and to whom exactly is it supposed to matter for? His point is that there is no common definition of SEPA, as demonstrated by some referring to it as the Single Euro Payments Area and others the Single European Payments Area.

There is no clarity of ownership, which is why there is no own-ership; there is no legal representation and the legislation meant to provide clarification is unclear; there is no business case for SEPA with users, the ACHs, the corporations or the banks and, where there is a business case such as with e-invoicing, it has nothing to do with SEPA.

All in all, it is just a political need that is driving SEPA and nothing else. So what is SEPA? No-one knows, so how can it matter?

Bob then opened the evening to an open discussion with the audience, who asked intriguing questions, such as: "where are the imperatives for SEPA? What will make this happen?" and put the provocative point, such as: "SEPA doesn't matter because there are far more important things taking over the agenda today, like Obama's banking reforms, balance sheet capitalisation and liquidity".

I think my favourite comment had to be from one panel member though, which was that SEPA seems to be moving in ever decreasing circles "having started with a vision and ended with a committee".

Anyways, we concluded the evening with a vote and, surprisingly, the motion was carried by a single vote.

So yes, this house does believe that SEPA matters ... just.

Are you taking the PSD? (2010)

Interesting article on the guide to all things Europe, Euractiv, about the Payment Services Directive.

The Directive "has been transposed in all but 11 of the 31 EU/ EEA countries".

Hmmm ... that would be Cyprus, Estonia, Italy and Latvia (Jan); Norway (Feb); Belgium, Greece, Spain, Finland, Malta and Poland (Mar); whilst Sweden is last (Apr).

> "Observers agree that it favours banks and card companies over the merchants, retailers and consumers who will be using the scheme."

Hmmm ... would the banks agree? The banks that have spent eight years pulling SEPA together? The banks that have spent billions on change and lost billions of margin? The banks that have been arguing that there is no benefit to merchants, retailers and consumers being communicated by the Commission or public authorities?

"The directive may lead to more fragmentation."

That's the point, isn't it?

By introducing new payments institutions, it creates more competition which leads to lower prices which leads to better markets, is the contention of the legislators. This was the same view with the other Directive, the Markets in Financial Instruments Directive, that led to market fragmentation for investing with the rise of Chi-X, BATS and many dark pool investment vehicles, where things are traded outside the line of sight of the public market.

Markets do fragment thanks to these Directives. Over time, they then consolidate. That is why Chi-X stands out as a clear leader in the post-MiFID trading world and, over time, the same will happen in the post-PSD payments world. So fragmentation isn't necessarily a long-term issue, but a short-term concern.

"The PSD's weaknesses lie in its opt-outs".

Absolutely. Check out our research if you want to know what they mean as derogations and opt-outs have created a truly uneven playing field for payments.

"Card companies argue that the EU's new rules do not address the issue of catching fraudulent transactions."

In the words of an old Tina Turner song:

"what's fraud got to do with it?"

The card companies are right, by the way. The PSD is purely concerned about moving towards a level playing field for payments in terms of the legal structures of cross-border transactions. The focus was primarily around direct debit and credit transfer operations, as this is where SEPA had focused and needed

121

support. Cards were not centre of the radar for the legislation, nor was fraud. Watch out for the PSD II in 2012 however, when these things do move to centre stage.

Postnote:

At the end of the article is the line:

> "SEPA is being treated as a low-priority project in Sweden and Finland because their respective ministries of finance have limited resources to roll out the scheme, according to Elemar Tertak from the European Commission."

I think the person who wrote this mistook PSD for SEPA.

40 days of the PSD (2009)

It's 40 days since the introduction of the Payment Services Directive (PSD), so there has been lots of chat about the PSD this week, and how it's working or not working.

Derogations and interpretations are rife, with the hottest and most contentious issue being the fact that charges are now meant to be shared (SHA in the SWIFT message exchange), except that many banks, institutions and even government administrations are insisting on OUR charging structures, where the sending bank pays all fees.

This issue is even causing ambiguity within a country, where one bank might accept OUR message payments from corporate clients in order to save the client having to re-jig their systems to accommodate, whilst another bank might not.

Even worse is where a bank sends a payment and gets a call from the beneficiary's bank saying that they will process it as SHA but, if the client objects to the charges, then they will process it as OUR and ask the sending bank to pay the fee plus a potential 'lifting fee'.

Elsewhere, some banks are taking the payments as SHA but then wrapping charges into other services and fees, so that the client does not realise they are paying or how much.

All of these shenanigans are just mere 'teething troubles' of course, as the PSD settles into the markets.

In fact, according to Ruth Wandhöfer, EMEA Head of Payments Strategy and Market Policy for Treasury & Trade Solutions at Citi's Global Transaction Services and member of the EU Banking Council for the PSD, there are things that are being captured and changed. For example, some German banks were asking for €170 to process an incoming cross-border direct debit payment because their systems are so inefficient. This has been slapped down, with a maximum of €40 being viewed as an acceptable charge (that's still high if you ask me). Equally, some Spanish banks were asking for 4% of any transaction as their fee. That's been slapped down too.

All in all, it is still clear that we have passed the start date for the PSD but the PSD has yet to start. For example, here's the state of transposition of the PSD according to the latest EU analysis:

What this shows is that Estonia, Greece, Latvia, Poland, Slovakia, Finland, Cyprus, Lithuania, Italy, Spain, Sweden and Belgium (Belgium!!!), all missed the deadline of 1st November 2009. This is poor form as that means only 15 of the EU27 made it on time. Only in September, when I last checked the Europa website for the state of play, they had confidently predicted that 26 countries would meet the deadline.

Even worse, those that are making the deadlines are misinterpreting, adding or changing the intent of the text. These changes take one of three forms:

◆ Derogations;

◆ Gold-plating;

◆ Divergence.

In the first instance, there are 23 derogations in the PSD. These are meant to allow each member state the ability to introduce the PSD without having to completely reinvent their payments infrastructures within country.

However, they are also creating major confusion, with the one derogation cited most often being the definitions of what is a microenterprise and how is it treated.

The UK classes microenterprises – small businesses – as consumers, and gives them all the rights and protections, products and services that would be afforded to a consumer in a payments transaction context. France, Spain and Italy, amongst others, use the derogation to classify microenterprises as corporates, and give them the rights and protections and products and services of a corporate client.

By doing this, they can offer and operate a consumer product as a corporate product under the PSD's definitions, with the most obvious standout being the Italians who claim that the Riba – a direct debit in any other country – is actually a corporate product and therefore not subject to the PSD's definitions of direct debits.

Gold-plating is also rife, particularly illustrated by the leg-in and leg-out dialogue where some countries are making themselves more attractive for payments processing by including US dollars and other non-EU currencies in their PSD definitions.

Finally, divergence is being created across countries by using definitions in different ways. For example, Belgium and Slovakia have used derogations to enable their markets to define the payments cycle to be same day, rather than the D+1 (or +3) as dictated by the PSD; meanwhile the UK, by clever interpretation of value dating rules, has managed to get around this completely.

No wonder this is all so confusing.

Anyways, to clarify the confusion, Ruth Wandhöfer presented some interesting insights, and here are a few of her bullet points ...

What is the PSD?

◆ The PSD represents a legal framework for payments within the European Union Single Market, covering the EU 27 as well as Norway, Iceland, Lichtenstein (not Switzerland!).

◆ The PSD is a European Directive, which means that all Member States were required to implement PSD rule into their national legislation, a process called transposition, by the deadline of the 1st November 2009.

◆ The PSD applies to payment transactions in euro and all other Member State currencies within the Single Market, where those are provided by payment service providers located in this Community.

◆ The PSD covers all electronic payment services, while cash to cash transactions and cheques are exempted from the scope.

◆ The PSD does not intend to cover payment services associated with securities asset servicing.

◆ The PSD's focus is on customer protection (not just consumer protection), covering the relationship between all providers and users of payments services.

◆ With the aim of enhancing competition the PSD creates a new lightly regulated entity called a "Payments Institution", allowing non-banks to handle payments and join the bankers' payment schemes and associations.

◆ The PSD also defines conduct of business rules for all payment service providers covering the end to end payer to payee relationship.

◆ The PSD will have a revolutionary impact on the legal framework between banks and their customers setting

125

stringent rules for information disclosure, conduct of business rules and service provision

- Harmonised refund rules have been established to support SEPA Direct Debits, while unique identifier primacy ensures for enhanced levels of straight-through-processing.

- Central Bank Reporting requirements for Euro transactions across the EEA still constitute a barrier to the free flow of SEPA transactions.

- Every credit institution that provides payment services in the EEA will have to comply with PSD's conduct of business rules.

Short-term issues with the PSD

- Banking industry and Commission were strongly in favour of all countries transposing the PSD for 1/11/09 given intra EU/EEA cross-border payments are in scope.

- In reality, the following countries are understood to have not been ready for the 1 November 2009 deadline: Estonia, Greece, Latvia, Poland, Slovakia, Finland, Cyprus, Lithuania, Italy, Spain, Sweden and Belgium. Spain and Slovakia joined in early December 09.

- Consequent impact in practical terms: clients may experience a brief period of non-uniform treatment where a 'PSD payment' is being sent to a country yet to complete its transposition; and hence where 'old' legal regime practices could be applied.

- An ideal 'best practice' would be if banks in late countries could voluntarily adopt key PSD payment processing provision (e.g. full amount principle) between 1/11/09 and transposition completion, but this may not always be possible.

126

- To help minimise uncertainty, the EU banking industry within the PSD Expert Group is looking to establish Best Practice Guidelines designed to establish an approach in the key countries where transposition was delayed to ensure broad principles of the PSD are nevertheless complied with (e.g. the 'no deduction' principle).

Full amount principle and charging options

- General rule: no deductions of charges allowed from the full amount where both legs of the payment are in the EEA and the transaction is in Euro or another Member State currency.

- EU Commission Services are strongly of the view that charges code SHA is the clear requirement in line with the charge sharing principle in Article A52(2) (excepting in cases where there is a currency exchange) – despite the slightly broader interpretation in a few Member States (who have not ruled out use of OUR option).

- The Commission and Banking industry further support a general move to using the 'SHA' charge code for all EEA currency payments travelling within the EEA.

- The usage of SHA will ensure that the 'full amount' of the payment transaction will travel up to the beneficiary bank and a separate fee agreed with the beneficiary client will be charged or deducted (in a transparent way from the full amount).

- Generally, the recommended best practice to all beneficiary banks is not to reject an incoming payment just on the grounds that the charge code is possibly 'inappropriate' as generally the beneficiary bank will not have all the facts necessary to make such a determination with certainty.

127

There were lots of other discussions about this during the week, but far too much to blog about every nuance of every chat. Suffice to say, my own bottom line is that this ain't working. Roll on the PSD II.

More on the SEPA DD launch (2009)

Just got an email from Charlie McCreevy's office that announces the launch of SEPA Direct Debits (SDD). Here's the official line:

> "Cross-border direct debits and easier bank account switching now possible

> "From the beginning of November, EU consumers will start to have the possibility to make regular payments using the new Single Euro Payments Area SEPA Direct Debit scheme, and should find it easier to switch their current account from one bank to another within their own Member State.

> "The new SEPA Direct Debit scheme means that, for the first time, consumers and businesses will be able to make direct debit transactions between different countries in the euro area. Direct Debits are a convenient way for consumers to make recurring payments and an efficient method for companies to collect money such as bills for water, gas, electricity and telecom services as well for magazine and periodical subscriptions. Although direct debits are widely used in many euro area countries, at present, there is no pan-European scheme in place for making these payments possible across borders. Supporting the industry-led scheme are new EU rules on payment services and cross-border payments, in force as of 1 November, which are designed to ensure that

SEPA Direct Debits will be as easy, efficient and secure as national schemes without being more expensive. Thousands of euro area banks have already signed up for the new scheme.

"The improvements in bank account switching are thanks to a set of 'Common Principles' adopted by the European Banking Industry Committee (EBIC) last year and have now been implemented in the Member States by the national banking associations. From now on, whenever consumers wish to switch their current account to another bank, the new bank will offer its assistance throughout the switching process."

Charlie McCreevy is then quoted as saying:

"Thanks to industry's efforts and a solid legal platform at EU level, direct debit payments can now be made between different countries in the euro area – good news for consumers, for businesses and for the economy as a whole.

"I am pleased that national banking associations have taken their self-regulatory agreement seriously and worked to ensure that the Common Principles on Bank Account Switching are ready to be applied by 1 November."

I would question some of the views here based upon the other official EU website, Euractiv, saying that banks and users have not bought into SEPA yet and our own research which demonstrates that the 'solid legal platform' is not solid at all.

But good on you for 'bigging it up', Charlie, as they say here in Chavland.

Today is SEPA day, wa-hey! (2009)

So, finally, November 2nd and here we are.

SEPA day!

SEPA direct debits go live today and the PSD was transposed successfully across all of Europe to become law yesterday.

Apart from a few countries who missed the deadline. Obviously, Sweden who have always said April because the chap who was meant to transpose it left. But did I hear Poland, Estonia and Greece are late? And who said Portugal, Spain and Italy? And what's that about Belgium in February, Finland in May?

Oh yes, and even if the authorities are late in transposing in each nation, there's also a lot of cynicism amongst the institutions. of course.

Many "banking and consumer associations say they have serious concerns that SEPA will open the way for more fraud and unfair pricing on payments", and "only 2,600 of Europe's 8,000 banks will be ready for the launch of SEPA's direct debit scheme on 2 November" according to Euractiv.

Our own recent research found Europe to be a land of payments confusion, with 58% of the 350 survey respondents saying that the PSD is being transposed inconsistently and 63% stating that this is because of different interpretations at the country level; only 13% believe it is being implemented correctly.

No wonder Elemer Tertak, director of financial institutions at the European Commission, said: "SEPA is a slow burner, not a chain reaction."

Too right.

Meanwhile, in a conversation with Craig Ramsey of ACI Worldwide and Jonathan Williams of Experian Payments, we got into some idea of how this may play out.

Q: What does the launch of SEPA DD mean for the future of the Eurozone?

Craig: The launch of SEPA Direct Debits is a continuation of politicians' desire for a single euro economy. It marks the next step of the SEPA initiative. However, in the greater scheme of things this introduction of SDD is unlikely to have a major impact on the way that people do business or who they bank with. Most of the customers that had a cross-border payment issue have already positioned themselves to reduce their costs.

Q: Why has there been such a delay and below-expected industry take up SEPA?

Jonathan: The key challenge here is the lack of added-value which is preventing corporate customers from migrating. At the recent Sibos conference in Hong Kong, Andrew Long from HSBC stated that customers need SEPA to be relevant to them to create demand and then migration. He suggested that SEPA was driven only by politicians and that we as an industry should find out what the market wants and then tailor the rules to fit. If SEPA was perceived as a value-added alternative there might have been less debate and no need for an enforced end date as customers would want to migrate.

Disagreements around interchange fees have also been a further setback for the European payments framework, culminating in French Banking Federation (FBF) suspending work on SEPA payment services.

For corporates who are already finding it difficult to see the benefits of SEPA, the discussion around interchange fees is likely to mean higher transaction costs, an unappealing prospect in the current economic downturn.

The lack of awareness around the SEPA migration requirements also stretches to conversion from domestic account numbering systems to the European BIC and IBAN system.

It is still clear that national legacy systems will be a barrier to take-up which means that few banks and their corporate customers are likely to be prepared for SEPA and some of the obstacles associated with the conversion from the Basic Bank Account Number (BBAN) to IBANs. However, by cleansing and validating BBAN details before conversion into IBANs and by validating existing IBANs on the database, both banks and corporates will be able to get around some of the hurdles in migrating to SEPA and truly herald the arrival of the scheme.

So what have we learnt from this? Who should take responsibility for governance of the initiative? Who should be responsible for developing and implementing the standards and systems needed? The answers to these questions are not clear with the European Commission proposing a new governance structure for SEPA and the project not yet nearing completion.

Q: Do we need stricter deadlines for SEPA migration?
Jonathan: The confusion about the timeframes for an end-date of legacy payment systems added to the lack of interest and urgency regarding implementation of the SEPA framework on the side of banks and corporates alike. Only setting a fixed end-date can provide the impetus needed to force the financial services industry into motion. While we can at least agree on what we mean by an end-date – the time when all domestic clearing has moved across to SEPA standards – there are still disagreements over how to address the country variations, or "additional optional services", perceived to be necessary to migrate domestic clearing harmoniously.

Q: How will it change the way we pay when it is here?
Craig: If you are a customer in the Eurozone, the launch could encourage the use of Direct Debits. However the trend towards electronic payments from traditional schemes will not be advanced by SEPA, as it is already happening regardless.

132

Q: What are the benefits and opportunities?
Jonathan: SEPA is bringing markets closer together and increasing cross-border opportunities for corporate organisations and banks alike. SEPA Direct Debits in particular will enable direct debit originators to collect pan-European direct debits from any of the SEPA countries using a single direct debit service instead of the country-specific services that currently exist. For banks and corporates the SEPA initiative will provide opportunities to improve end-to-end straight-through processing, reduce processing and transaction costs and expand markets. Those planning to make use of the initiative will benefit from greater efficiency in terms of consolidating their systems and rationalising the number of bank accounts they hold as well as having a common standard for direct debit transactions in Euro countries. Those corporates which need to make payments to and receive payments from the European Economic Area will benefit from this more standardised approach to payment transactions.

Q: What does it mean for banks?
Craig: Banks have had to spend a lot of money preparing for the launch of SEPA Direct Debits without a strong business case and with no guaranteed return on investment. However, the launch date itself will not have a large effect while an end-date for migration to SEPA products from legacy products will have a much greater impact. In the short term, they will have to support both SEPA products and legacy products simultaneously, which will be an extra strain on profit margins. At least once an end-date is set, banks will be able to plan the move away from supporting multiple products.

Q: What does it mean for payment processors?
Craig: Certain aspects of SEPA Direct Debits are commodities that banks could potentially buy in from payments proces-

sors. This could add further business viability for banks to move towards outsourcing and cloud computing business models.

PSD and SEPA research results (2009)

Our research results into the PSD and SEPA are officially released today, with the press release below.

European payments: a land of confusion

London, September 8th, 2009

Major research project reveals the flaws in Europe's ambitions

European payments are about to be dramatically changed through a new European Directive for Payments and the completion of the Single Euro Payments Area scheme for direct debits, but there are alarming differences in country interpretations and implementation, as revealed by the largest research study of this market to date.

With the Payment Services Directive (PSD) due to come into force on 1st November 2009 and the Single Euro Payments Area (SEPA) Direct Debit (SDD) scheme to follow on 2nd November, Europe should be at the start of a transparent, harmonised and integrated market for payments and payment processing. Instead, Europe's policymakers, banks, corporates and infrastructure providers have become increasingly frustrated with 58% of them saying that the PSD is being transposed inconsistently and 63% stating that this is because of different interpretations at the country level. Only 13% believe it is being implemented correctly, according to a major European research report published today by The Financial Services Club, sponsored by BT, Earthport and Logica.

The research surveyed over 350 global payments professionals about SEPA and the PSD's progress, as well as conducting over 25 in-depth interviews with the key organisations involved, including the European Commission, European Central Bank, European Payments Council, Euro Banking Association and European Association of Corporate Treasurers, as well as leading banks, infrastructures, payment institutions, corporates, vendors, consultancies and more.

In particular, the following personnel agreed to be quoted in the final report, for which we thank them:

◆ Ashley Dowson, Chairman, the SEPA Consultancy;

◆ Daniele Danese, Payments Manager, Banco Populari de Verona;

◆ Dermot Nolan, Head of Payments Strategy, Planning & Change, Bank of Ireland;

◆ Frank Taal, General Manager, Wholesale Banking Product Management, Payments and Cash Management, ING;

◆ Gerard Hartsink, Chairman, European Payments Council;

◆ Gianfranco Tabasso, Chairman, the European Association of Corporate Treasurers (EACT);

◆ Gilbert Lichter, Chief Executive, EBA;

◆ Harry Newman, Head of Banks and Payments Market Infrastructures, SWIFT;

◆ Jad Khallouf, Chief Executive, STET;

◆ Lázaro Campos, Chief Executive, SWIFT;

◆ Leon Isaacs, Chief Executive, the International Association of Money Transfer Networks (IAMTN);

◆ Martin O'Donovan, Technical Director, the Association of Corporate Treasurers;

- Martin Wilson, Chief Commercial Officer, VocaLink;

- Massimo Battistella, Manager, Accounts Receivables, Administration, Finance & Control, Telecom Italia;

- Michael Steinbach, Chairman, Equens;

- Paul Smee, Chief Executive, UK Payments Council;

- Vincent Brennan, Head of Group Payments, Bank of Ireland;

- Werner Steinmuller, Head of Global Transaction Services, Deutsche Bank.

The conclusion of the research is that European member states are implementing the Payment Services Directive in a completely inconsistent manner which threatens to derail the progress of the Single Euro Payments Area. Certain member states were particularly cited as at issue more than others, with Germany and Italy seen to be a particular issue. Sweden is also at issue, as it cannot implement the PSD until April 2010 due to skills issues.

On a more positive note, participants do expect new payments institutions to gain market share, particularly money transfer service providers, and that these changes have motivated many banks to look for more innovative services for their clients, particularly around corporate information services, e-payments, m-payments and e-invoicing.

Overall, the findings suggest that Europe's payments program is moving in the right direction, but is still too slow and fragmented to achieve the objectives of true harmonisation without more co-ordination and management between the Commission, ECB and EPC, with the member states banks, policymakers, corporations and citizens.

For example, Werner Steinmuller, Head of Global Transaction Services for Deutsche Bank, states that:

"Efficient markets need efficient payments systems. If it's not happening, then it's a crossroad for SEPA and the PSD, that may stop these changes succeeding."

Chris Skinner, Chairman of the Financial Services Club and leader of the research project, adds:

"European payment initiatives have come a long way over the past seven years, in the bid to achieve a harmonised financial market.

However, the time, cost and gradual process has slowed to the point of boredom and frustration for many involved and there is now a big concern that a further period of static vacuum, as the PSD irons out its inconsistencies, could undermine the achievements of the SEPA program."

Key findings

◆ 58% of survey respondents say that the PSD is being transposed inconsistently and 63% state that this is because of different interpretations at the country level; only 13% believe it is being implemented correctly.

◆ 64% of banks and 67% of infrastructure providers believe the interpretation at country level is an issue.

◆ 61% of respondents believe this program is 'critical' (18%) or 'very important' (43%) to Europe's future.

◆ 35% believe the benefits are that it will make European commerce 'seamless and simple, with less banks and fewer barriers to cross border trade', whilst 18% felt the major benefit was to 'allow international corporations to rationalise their bank relationships', and 13% that it would create a Eurozone as 'large and competitive as America or China'.

◆ 14% said the main driver of the harmonisation program is for the 'benefits', with 19% voting for the 'cost savings' and 15% for 'increased competition'; but the single largest group were the 38% who believe this is purely 'politics' being driven out by the European Commission's agenda.

♦ 58% of Germans saying it is political compared to 23% of Italians. Equally, 42% of the banks state it is political compared to 25% of the technology firms. In fact, the only group that had a wildly different view were those from outside Europe, with 23% of the non-European voters believing that the changes are focused upon 'benefits' and 18% for 'innovations'.

♦ 37% of respondents believe the biggest barrier to the PSD's success is 'national protectionism'.

♦ 28% of respondents say their banks are leading the way or being supportive of SEPA, and a further 55% say their banks are implementing SEPA according to the rules; 17% believe their banks are either avoiding or delaying SEPA.

♦ 21% of this survey's respondents think that the date for the SEPA vision to be fully realised could be as soon as 2012, but most think sometime thereafter with 23% saying 2015 and 11% sometime after 2018.

When asked why SEPA Credit Transfers (SCT) are taking so long to take off, the clear answer (27% of respondents) is that it is because there is no motivation because there is no end-date. A further 22% felt it was because everyone is unsure of the benefits that can be gained from SCTs.

When asked who was most supportive of the SEPA agenda, bankers voted for the European Commission (46%) first, rather than themselves (27%).

When asked: "how ready are your banks for the implementation of SDDs in your country?"

- Belgium: 13 out of 15 respondents said ready (87%);
- Germany: 20 out of 24 respondents said ready (83%);
- Austria: 10 out of 12 respondents said ready (83%);
- Italy: 10 out of 12 respondents said ready (83%);
- Spain: 6 out of 8 respondents said not ready (75%);
- Ireland: 11 out of 18 respondents said not ready (61%);
- Sweden: 4 out of 8 respondents said not ready (50%);
- France: 4 out of 8 respondents said not ready (50%);
- UK: 36 out of 78 respondents said not ready (46%);
- Netherlands: 4 out of 9 respondents said not ready (44%).

When asked: "How well prepared do you believe your national authorities are for the implementation of the Payment Services Directive on 1st November 2009?" the survey found that only 15% of country-based respondents felt their country was 'very ready'; 23% felt 'quite ready'; 30% 'just about ready; 27%, 'not really ready'; and 6% 'not ready at all'.

When asked: "How is your country implementing the PSD?"

- 7% of respondents say their country is implementing the full PSD with no changes;
- 60% state they are implementing the full PSD with changes that are permitted;
- 19% are implementing part of the PSD, but the important parts (10% with no changes and 9% with changes that are permitted);
- 10% are transposing with changes that are not permitted; and
- 4% are not implementing the PSD at all.

Conclusions

The Payment Services Directive is flawed in both its drafting and transposition.

The 23 Additional Optional Services (AOS) along with derogations (the ability to interpret legal terms for local implementation) mean that member states have inconsistencies over how currencies are treated and whether they are in or out of PSD's coverage (the 'leg-in' / 'leg-out' issue); how small businesses are classified as consumers or corporates; how payment accounts are defined; how direct debit products are defined; and more.

Every country is using AOS and derogation to protect historical products, services and infrastructures.

This inconsistency means that there is no harmonisation across Europe's payments instruments, even though this is a maximum harmonisation directive.

It is highly likely that 2012, when the European Commission review the transposition and implementation of the PSD, that a revised PSD will be drafted eliminating AOS and other anomalies, such as multilateral interchange fees on cross-border direct debits.

The result is that the PSD will not support an integrated and harmonised European payments marketplace until 2013 or beyond.

The Single Euro Payments Area is progressing but too slowly.

SEPA's clearly gained momentum as banks convert core systems to use the new schemes and formats; by way of example, SEPA Credit Transfers have more than doubled in volume from under 2% of all credit transfers in the Eurozone in May 2009 to almost 5% by August 2009.

SEPA is still progressing far too slowly to be convincing however, and when SEPA Direct Debits come into play in November 2009, if the new schemes are not demonstrating critical mass within an 18-month timeframe, then the SEPA program will be deemed to have failed

SEPA has strong support amongst the banking community, but not amongst corporates and other end-users; this support needs to be promoted through political weight of force by ensuring all member state public authorities and utilities migrate to the use of SEPA instruments during 2010 and by the introduction of an end-date for SEPA migration as a regulatory mandate.

The SEPA end-date is expected to be around the end of 2013, but the migration of end users (corporates) and obsolescence of existing national infrastructures is not expected to happen until the end of the next decade (2018 or thereafter).

Ultimately, Europe's payments program is definitely off course. How far off course is just dependent upon which way you look at it.

The total view on SEPA and the PSD (2009)

At the payments conference I attended last week, a major theme was the PSD and SEPA.

Summarising the PSD and SEPA areas makes for interesting reading, and builds upon the two entries I made last week about the show titled "SEPA may not happen", and "Quantifying views on SEPA".

Anyways, back to the overall industry views and, in the first major discussion about SEPA and the PSD, Daniela Umstätter – the National Expert in Retail Issues, Consumer Policy and Payment Systems for the DG Internal Market at the European Commission – said that they were "not very happy" with the lack of progress on migration to SEPA Credit Transfers.

Money for Nothing and your Cheques for Free

"The financial crisis has had an impact, but we need SEPA now than ever because it will bring harmonisation and standards that will allow banks to realise cost efficiencies."

Delegates seemed to agree, 50% of them having voted that the market crisis put more emphasis on achieving full migration to SEPA. Moreover, the majority (54%) felt current delivery channels and bank payment products were inadequate in the new Internet and mobile world.

The EC is working on two papers to help support the migration to SEPA: an Action Plan that addresses the issues raised by the financial crisis will be published soon, along with a separate consultation paper on a SEPA end date.

Wiebe Ruttenberg, Head of the Market Integration Division, European Central Bank, said an end date would give a great deal of clarity. An end date would likely be around 2013, which five years after the introduction of SCTs should fit into most financial institutions' investment cycles. Seventy per cent of delegates said a single end date set by EU regulatory authorities was necessary in order to achieve migration from legacy payments instruments to SEPA instruments.

Ruttenberg mounted a sturdy defence of the PSD and SEPA, telling delegates that there was a change in payment behaviour ahead and that if instruments were not developed in the "right way" or aren't adopted, banks will be like dinosaurs and will die out. "We need one European space for doing payments. Banks can build on the basic SCT, SDD and SEPA Cards instruments, combining them with online, mobile and e-invoicing services. There is an expectation that banks will provide the most attractive service offerings for customers, if they don't there are others who will step in."

When challenged that SDDs would be inferior to existing domestic instruments, Ruttenberg said the ECB and EC's assessment of the situation was that differences could be solved through

Additional Optional Services. "We shouldn't forget that SEPA is about European integration. We have a solution, and while not everyone is happy with it, it is a solution that can be offered on a European level."

Ruttenberg also updated delegates on SCT volumes, which have risen to 2.9% since the migration on to SCTs by Slovenia's new ACH. Subsequent speakers made play of the fact that one year on from their introduction SCT volumes were so low, speculating that at the current rate of growth it would take anything up to 100 years to get full adoption. However, Gilbert Lichter, Chief Executive EBA Clearing Co and Secretary General of the Euro Banking Association, said such critics ignored the network effect of growth. SCT traffic was growing at 15–20% per month, he said, and it would take a considerably shorter time to see full migration.

Gerard Hartsink, chairman of the European Payments Council said while the transposition of the PSD into national law was a concern of those who attended the most recent plenary session of the EPC, only Sweden had said it would not be ready. The industry was on track for the primary deliverables of the SDD and countries including Brazil, the US and Russia were interested in SEPA. "We will be delivering new services for customers based on better cooperation models, new standards, technology and infrastructure," he said.

SEPA implementation

In particular, there are issues with the SEPA model.

This was illustrated by two questions put to delegates at the start of the IPS 2009 sessions on SEPA implementation, that received overwhelming agreement: we need to create new cooperative models with the involvement of all market participants – banks, users, suppliers and regulators (70%); and we need to widen our vision of the types of services and infrastructures

Money for Nothing and your Cheques for Free

we should provide, such as e-billing, e-invoicing and supply chain data (75%).

Rob Jonker, Senior Product Manager, Global Payments, Deutsche Bank said the SEPA business case for corporates was still very minor. Large corporates do view SEPA as part of a bigger picture and potentially strategic, but the lack of an end date was a problem.

Mario de Lorenzo, Director of Payments Systems, SIA-SSB, said banks' payments architectures must evolve in order to optimise processes and reduce costs. Standards would enable innovative services to be developed that can increase revenues and reduce time to market.

A key message that emerged from the sessions on SEPA was the need for better communication between banks and corporates.

Ashley Dowson, Chairman of The SEPA Consultancy, said the leadership of the political agenda had "disappeared" during the past few years. "SEPA customers were excluded from discussions for too long and are now too vocal. There must be a balance between banks and their users. Banks need to stretch their budgets to provide the services that are required, but corporates mustn't request certain services merely to antagonise banks."

Martine Brachet, Head of Interbank Relationships, Payment Services Division, Société Générale reminded delegates that SDDs were very complex and "there will be many lessons to be learned in November when they become a reality". She also assured delegates that the French banking community had begun work on SDDs, having recently received clarification about multilateral interchange fees (MIFs). "The French banking community felt it was better to undertake all of the necessary preparation for SDDs before doing things we maybe could not manage." France has committed to introduce SDDs in November 2010.

The MIF issue was important when it came to SEPA for cards as well. Norbert Bielefeld, Deputy Director, Payments and Secu-

144

rities, European Savings Bank Group, World Savings Banks Institute, reminded delegates of the principles of MIFs. "Interchange was successful in building and developing the cards business. If one of the objectives of SEPA is to have market transformation, you cannot have that without continued innovation. It is very difficult to innovate without investment and without MIFs this will be a real challenge."

SEPA was introducing a more cooperative approach in the payments industry said Manfred Schuck, Executive Advisor to the Board of Directors at Equens. "Before SEPA was introduced, we had more than 30 different local infrastructures servicing only national markets. There will be a network community in the future comprised of partners. I think the number of infrastructure providers that will survive can be counted on the fingers of one hand."

Marc Niederkorn, Director, McKinsey and Co, said SEPA would happen – something that a year ago he would have said with more caution. "SEPA will encourage interesting new economic models because banks will need to cut costs and increase efficiency. I think we will see much more outsourcing of operations that are difficult to manage in-house, which is good news for the banks that can propose centralisation and network management."

Jad Khallouf, Chief Executive Officer, STET, said SEPA expectations had been mismanaged. "You have to face up to SEPA if you are to survive but it is a huge challenge. Corporates are not ready, not only because of the lack of an end date. Like banks, they are striving to survive in the current economic turmoil."

PSD implementation

With the PSD due to come into effect from 1 November this year, Ruth Wandhofer, Head of Payments Strategy, EMEA Global Transaction Services, Citi, said there were still a number of

Money for Nothing and your Cheques for Free

challenges with the PSD, particularly for banks operating in more than one country across Europe.

> "Most banks can tackle the customer communications aspect of the PSD at the last minute, but making the required system and procedure changes is more of a long-term project and some people are running slightly late on this."

The overriding message that came out of the day was that the PSD cannot be reversed and financial institutions need to deal with it. As Dermot Turing, Partner, International Financial Institutions and Markets Group at Clifford Chance said: "It's too late to argue about the content of the PSD. What law firms need to do now is help to interpret the PSD in a consistent way that minimises system and client-facing burdens."

Daniela Umstätter, National Expert, Retail Issues, Consumer Policy and Payment Systems DG, European Commission said she was puzzled that uncertainty remained in the market about the transposition of the PSD into national law. "We are well on track with the PSD. Only one state, Sweden, has a problem with transposition and we will be helping them out. In general, the PSD is a fully harmonised directive, there is no room for interpretation and where there is, we are trying to solve it."

John Burns, Senior Associate Retail Policy, Financial Services Authority had an uncompromising view: "The industry says complying with the PSD is difficult. We understand that, but the law is there and will have to be dealt with. Saying it is difficult doesn't get us beyond what the law is."

The PSD does present difficulties to banks, particularly those that operate in more than one country. Only the UK and Bulgaria have so far issued new payments laws based on the PSD. Concerns were raised about the treatment of leg-out transactions when no currency conversion was involved, what was meant by making funds immediately available, how to deal with late payments, charge codes for corporates, execution times for card payments and the impact of being non-compliant.

Bjorn Flismark, Senior Vice President, Global Transaction Services, SEB said the PSD changes a great deal for banks, imposing rules where previously they were used to doing "what they wanted or what they thought they could get away with". Complying with D+1 on payments would require banks to consider new business models and how to charge customers in the future. "Those that have relied on float income in the past will be asking how they can replace this." However, once systems have been changed "at a terrible cost", banks will in the longer term enjoy cheaper processing and simpler rules to live by.

Martin O'Donovan, Assistant Director, Policy and Technical, Association of Corporate Treasurers said from a corporate perspective, whether it takes one or three days for a payment to arrive is not crucial; having certainty is. The possibility of corporate opt-outs from certain provisions is being discussed among corporate treasurers and O'Donovan said many treasurers were taking stock of banking services and how they differ from country to country. "We are advising our members to ensure that they understand what they have so they can talk to banks in a meaningful way about opt-outs."

Changes in law don't make for a new market, it is business opportunities that do, Dr Thaer Sabri, Chief Executive, Electronic Money Association, reminded delegates. "If the PSD creates opportunities for a deluge of new payment institutions to come on to the market you would have to ask are these business opportunities that banks have left open? Money remitters, merchant acquirers and some third-party processors may all see opportunities in extending services. At the same time, some banks might hive-off their payments businesses and create specialist subsidiaries."

Participants in the boot camp were left in little doubt that the PSD would have a significant impact on their payments operations. And as Burns pointed out, with countries outside the EU and EEA looking at the PSD, it may well be that in the future representatives from financial institutions elsewhere in the world will be mulling over the same questions.

Corporates and SEPA

There were mixed messages from corporate treasurers regarding their attitudes and readiness for SEPA and the PSD.

Raffi Basmadjian, Head of Group Cash Management and Head of IT for Group Treasury, France Telecom Group Treasury, said the firm was collecting BICs and IBANs, but with many millions of customers, this was proving to be a significant problem. However, he said SEPA would give France Telecom homogeneity within a group of standards and channels. "All treasury operations will be performed in the same way from one country to another." The company's next step is to centralise domestic collection systems with a collections factory and local payment systems into a payments factory. Andreas Resei, European Treasurer at Mondi Group, said SEPA could be a catalyst for larger treasury projects within the organisation.

Gianfranco Tabasso, Chief Executive of FMS Group on the other hand, said Italian corporates were not ready for SEPA and would not begin to get ready until there was an end date. "Large companies are aware of SEPA but are also waiting for the PSD transposition in order to change their customer contracts."

Massimo Battistella, Manager of Accounts Receivables, Administration Services at Telecom Italia said he was concerned about the risk in SEPA instruments and some of their business models. "Italian corporates are working with the banking system to develop AOS in order to have instruments that better fit our requirements."

Quantifying people's views on SEPA (2009)

The International Payments Summit was attended by around 300 people, mostly bankers and payments solutions providers from across Europe. Throughout the conference, interactive electronic voting was used to gauge people's views of the markets, the economic crisis and the implementation of SEPA.

Here are the results.

The first question was:

What is the value of transaction services (payments processing) to a bank?

> 32.7% A stable source of revenue
>
> 25.5% An anchor product for the bank to keep the customer
>
> 23.6% Provides infrastructure for enabling financial processes
>
> 5.5% Other

Ah, so perhaps the view that banks view payments processing as a way to lock in customers is right. After all, money transmissions are the core of a bank's services aren't they?

What is your most pressing area for near-term focus in 2009?

> 38.2% New revenue sources
>
> 22.4% Regulations
>
> 19.7% Risk management
>
> 15.8% Cost reduction
>
> 3.9% Surviving

Interestingly the focus is finding growth, which is positive.

What is your most pressing area for longer-term?

82.89% New revenue sources

5.26% Regulations

3.95% Cost reduction

3.95% Surviving

I note here how risk management disappeared from the list. So risk is just a short-term focus whilst we get over this market blip?

Of the following, which are the most interesting areas in 2009?

54.23% SEPA and the Payment Services Directive

28.81% Remittances and mobile payments

15.75% Getting back to basics

1.69% MT202 Cover Payments

So over half the audience are focused upon SEPA and the PSD. Not surprising as it's a European audience and, in a separate voting sessions, the audience were asked specifically about their views of SEPA and the PSD's progress.

Is SEPA going to help Europe's Lisbon agenda for an integrated EU financial marketplace?

66.7% Yes

9.5% No

23.8% No idea

Around a quarter of attendees, most of whom specialise in payments in the EU, have no idea whether SEPA will help the Lisbon agenda to create a single European financial market. Interesting.

Who is going to benefit most from SEPA?

  33.33% Consumers

  46.97% Businesses

  12.12% Banks

  4.55% Public Authorities

  3.03% No idea

Apparently 84.85% of the audience were bankers and 12.12% corporate users. The other 3.03% were just confused.

Will the PSD be implemented homogeneously throughout Europe?

  26.1% Yes

  68.1% No

  5.8% No idea

The interactive voting finished with the general question:

When do you expect the turnaround to happen?

  1.5% Before summer 2009

  10.6% Second half 2009

  21.2% Early 2010

  28.8% Mid 2010

  28.8% Late 2010

  9.1% Later

Mmmm ... most are looking to 2010 or beyond. Seems to be a general consensus although 2010 for a turnaround means turning around from contraction to what?

  Flat-lining?
  Growth?
  Slow growth or fast growth?

Money for Nothing and your Cheques for Free

The danger that SEPA may not happen (2009)

I was invited to a conference this week and given the title of the talk as:

"Why there's a very real danger that SEPA may not happen".

As a good European who believes in the PSD and SEPA, I declined to discuss this and invited my long-time acquaintance Sir Jonathan Brit to speak on my behalf. Sir Jonathan "Johnny" Brit is the eighth generation of Brits to Chair Fusty Bank UK plc, which recently appeared in this blog talking about mobile telephones. He is one of the old guard, highly bigoted and patriotic, anti-European British people, normally referred to as an 'old fart' ... although not normally to his face.

I wrote most of his speech down to see what a typical British old fart thinks about SEPA. However, before you read his speech, please note that the views he expresses are not my own. For example, he seems to think that that it's purely a political plot by the French and Germans to take over Europe's financial infrastructures via the EBA and ECB respectively, which is why no-one has any urgency to implement. This is why nothing's happened yet, after 10 years, and that the lack of leadership, corporate inclusion, end-dates and more, means it is not working.

Meantime, over to you, Sir Jonathan.

Good afternoon. My name is Johnny Brit, Chairman of Fusty Bank UK plc.

Of course, we're not actually based in the UK for tax reasons, but it makes sense to have a registered office there as our people trust us more that way.

Now then, I've been asked here today to talk about this SEPA thing, which stands for Silly European Payments Agenda I believe. I've got to be careful when I say that, as I ran this past our PR and legal folks and they've made sure that everything I'm going to say is politically correct.

That's why I need to get some things out in the open before we start as I know that you all take this thing very seriously but I ask myself, after almost 10 years of all your faffing about trying to work out what it is, whether you are really serious about this stuff.

I don't think so.

Now we all know why, don't we?

Yes, because it's just a Stupid European Political Agenda isn't it?

This SEPA thing and all that stuff about a Payment Services Directive was only dreamed up by the poor political Eurocrats in Brussels because they couldn't pay for their books and cups of tea without incurring cross-border charges.

That's why this thing came about and that's why it's here.

It's nothing to do with saving costs and increasing efficiencies, which is what the politico's claim ... but only because that sounds good. No.

It's just to reduce their own unnecessary expenses of having to live in boring old Brussels whilst paying for a nice penthouse villa on the Riviera or chic bordello in Bermondsey.

That's the truth of it.

I know it's true, you know it's true, and as a political agenda we can pretty much ignore it can't we because, by the time they get around to realising we haven't done it, they'll no longer be MEPs and the new lot come in and we can mess them around too can't we.

Now certainly that's what we've been doing over here in Blighty – ignoring it that is – and I thought most of you European Johnnies had been doing the same, which is why nothing has happened.

But then I cannot believe how much of a dust-up there has been about this over the past 10 years.

Money for Nothing and your Cheques for Free

I mean, you've had conferences, meetings, committees, working parties, conventions ... you name it and you've had it. All about this silly euro thingy and these associated SEPA and PSD bits.

And for how long have you been doing this?

Ten years! Pwah! This all began ten years ago for God's sake and what have you got? Sure, there's been the Regulation 2560 which banned razor blades and biros. Sorry? Oh I didn't realise. I thought you said "I ban BIC", not IBAN BIC. Well, either way, IBANs and BICs haven't happened have they?

Certainly, most of the corporates we deal with haven't implemented these ... but that's because we do it for them as it is a sure-fire way to keep our business customers locked into the bank. In fact, I don't want them to change their SAP and ledger systems to work with IBANs and BICs as they will then have portability of their bank account.

That may be what the Eurocrats want, but I don't want that so they can just go and stuff their standards up their rears, as I'm keeping my customers locked into Account Numbers and Sort Codes. We'll handle the IBAN and Biccies.

I guess that is why, after 10 years, less than 2% of all potential Eurozone credit transfer payments are migrated onto these new SEPA Credit Transfer services, as there is no critical mass or need for this amongst the people we serve.

Funnily enough, fewer than 2% of all credit transfer volumes in 15 months would mean that to get to the total market space SEPA is meant to reach would take 100 years.

A century to achieve critical mass? Sounds about right to me as that means SEPA won't happen in my lifetime.

That's also why in 10 years, there's no legal structure in place, no movement of other electronic payments, and just an inconsistent idea that there might be some sort of standardised direct debit thingy.

154

Ten years and I think that you, like me, have just been ignoring this thing hoping that those Brussely Eurocrats will go away and stop worrying about their travels around Europe and bank fees.

Trouble is, they haven't gone away, have they?

That's why we are all eagerly waiting the Payment Services Directive in November or, as we call it, the Psssttt or the Okey-Kokey Directive. Y'know, you put your left leg-in and your right leg-out, so no-one knows which leg is which and then we can charge lots for it.

Now everyone thinks that we have all been waiting for the Psssttt, because then direct debits can come in on November 2nd and suddenly there will be lots and lots of volume. That's because all the businesses and authorities of Europe will place all their payments and transfers electronically through standardised systems and infrastructures.

Complete baloney, of course, as most of our corporate customers haven't been consulted about this. I mean, we did allow them in the room didn't we, but only as long as they didn't say anything or for as long as we could ignore them.

That's why corporates had no representation on any of our committees and discussion groups, but we are here to serve them of course ... just as long as we can keep them locked in to our bank and not someone else's.

So now we have these deadlines, with 1st November 2009 looming large as the date when things really things start ... but then things won't finish as we have no end dates, do we?

We have no end dates because no-one can agree on this euro thing – who's in and who's out – and because we have no leadership.

No-one is forcing this through because the leadership has to come from the politicians, and the politicians don't want to rock the boats in their home countries over something that's not a domestic issue.

After all, how many cross-border payments do we make? Less than 2%!

That's why the politicians don't want to upset their home countries and create a backlash.

The Germans may want SEPA as they have the European Central Bank but German banks don't want it because they have no central infrastructures; the French want it because the EBA is based in Paris and offer a PEACH, but French banks don't want it because it will damage their fee rates; the Italians are trying to work out what a Euro is; the Spanish are asleep and saying 'mañana'; and the rest of Europe are trying to work out what the hell the other guys are up to.

Meanwhile, the Dutch are leading the whole thing because they're the only people who speak the main languages of Europe. It would have been the Swiss otherwise, but they're not in Europe so they had to bow out by default.

Typical jolly European beanies.

And even with all of that, they can't agree.

I mean, the PSD is meant to be a hard deadline date for implementation by 1st November 2009 and the Swedish, who will have the Presidency of the European Union by then, have already said they cannot implement it. But at least the Swedish are honest, as the rest of the countries are just keeping quiet and pretending.

For example, look at the French.

They go and push for all this stuff and put all the infrastructure in Paris – yes, the EBA who run all this SEPA stuff, where are they based? Paris! And then, after all that, what do the French go and do? They say "non" and totally ignore it all.

Oh yes, and just in case you missed it this was the announcement of France not bothering with SEPA Direct Debits until November 2010.

Typical Français I say, especially as they announce this the day after the European Payments Council agreed all the banks of

Europe would have these direct debity thingies in place by November 2009.

Sacre bleu, mon dieu and grande m*rde.

Anyways, the French SEPA Committee, made up of the Banque de France and the French Banking Federation, are probably following Monsieur Sarkozy's lead and thought: "C*sse-toi". And at least I've read "La Princesse de Cleves".

Anyways, this is normal French thinking and short of bunging a few tractors across the Channel Tunnel to block electronic payments moving across borders, the French can only stick to their guns and try to ignore this silly political agenda.

Which brings me to another thing.

What is SEPA for anyway?

All it does is create a nice large zone for the Germans and French, who don't want it, to control the finances of the Spanish, Italians and rest, which is a good reason for not being in the euro isn't it?

I mean this SEPA thing is only good for two countries isn't it?

Sure, there are 16 countries in the Eurozone but, after the recent credit crisis, you've got the Germans controlling interest rates, the French controlling the infrastructure, and the Spanish, Italians and rest all suffering with crippling unemployment and stagnation with no hope of getting out of it.

That's why there are no end dates because we all want to keep our national infrastructures in place just in case. Just in case we have to go back to French francs, Italian lira, Spanish pesetas and Deutsche marks.

This is why we British are not in the Eurozone for very good reasons, the utmost of which is our right to retain our sovereignty. The Queen is very important to this island and represents our long heritage of ruling the world which is why everyone speaks English, even the French. So, we need to retain our sovereignty and stay out of the euro for this reason.

Money for Nothing and your Cheques for Free

In summary, after 10 years we've got a little bit of something and a lot of nothing.

No end dates, no leadership and no mandate to make this change happen.

Ten years! The Americans put a man on the moon in six years. Their moonshot was announced in 1963 and achieved in 1969. In six years, Americans can put a man on the moon and in Europe in 10 years we can't even get an agreement on a direct debit.

That's why we here in Fusty Bank UK plc are outsourcing all of our Eurozone payments to our trusted allies ... NACHA.

Thank you and goodbye.

Please note once again that the views expressed here are not my own but Johnny Brit's.

SEPA and the PSD aren't broken ... just irrelevant (2009)

Yesterday I said that SEPA and the PSD were irrelevant. I thought I better explain my logic in more depth, as this could offend some people.

It's not that SEPA and the PSD are irrelevant to you guys. If you're a payments plumbing person, which many of us are, it's very relevant. It's just that it's irrelevant to most corporates and businesses as to what we're doing with our plumbing.

For example, the euro was introduced through the Maastricht Treaty of 1992, became a currency in 1999, notes and coins in 2002 and a reserve currency at some point in mid-2007 as the dollar tanked.

The ECB and EBA were inaugurated in 1998 to prepare for the currency, and the PSD process began with the Lisbon Meeting of 2000 that resulted in the EPC being formed in 2002.

The SEPA Roadmap Vision began in 2002, and various rulebooks and processes were created by 2005 resulting in SEPA

Credit Transfers becoming reality in January 2008, with SEPA Direct Debits to follow by the end of 2009.

The EBA claims to be the PEACH with reach now, as long as you ignore Spain, and STEP1 became STEP2, although volumes are still pretty low. After all, the larger thick ACH's are processing almost 100 million transactions per day, whilst we're struggling to get volumes through STEP2 right now.

Of course, these things will change. It just takes a lot of time, as mentioned yesterday, to get all the parties involved to agree, commit and implement.

It's a push process, and most corporates are not interested until we get our act together.

On the other hand, let's look at something that happened during this period.

In December 1998, PayPal was launched and today, they have over 170 million users in over 190 countries in 19 currencies. Something like that anyways.

Now what strikes me as rather incongruous is that whilst we, as an industry, have debated and argued and dialogued and agreed and finally started to implement core critical plumbing for euro payments, in the same timeframe, a little upstart internet firm has become a global payments standard for low value electronic payments.

How come?

It's even more than that in fact. For example, using PayPal you can pretty much buy from anyone globally. I can buy goods in China, Asia, the USA and all across Europe if so desired, by just using PayPal. I had a client the other day who I owed €4,000. They are based in Amsterdam and I'm in London. My bank would charge me £25 to wire that over, and I had to go to the branch to authorise this ... or I can send them a cheque in £'s sterling which their bank then converts and charges ... or I could pay them exactly €4,000 via PayPal, which is what I did. It may cost me fees and percentages, but it was far cheaper and more cost effective time-wise, than using the banking system. So even small businesses can run pan-European payments services seamlessly across borders today, without worrying about SEPA and the PSD.

The fact is that this stuff is moving so fast that, for all of our deliberations, we are just far too slow.

By way of example, Barack Obama just became president-elect thanks to a great deal of charisma and a bucketful of cash. Of his $600 million war chest, $450 million came through online donations via his websites, and also fan pages on Facebook, MySpace and other social networks.

In September alone, Obama raised $150 million through just over 630,000 donations averaging $100 each, and 1.5 million Americans joined his social network, mybarackobama.com.

McCain didn't stand a chance and the out-of-touch Republican campaign reminds me of our SEPA and PSD programme, compared to the dynamic Democrat campaign that rings more of PayPal and friends.

In 2004, when the last American election occurred, no-one had heard of MySpace, Facebook or even YouTube. YouTube hit most people's radar when Google paid $1.5 billion for them in October 2006.

Most of us were unaware of Facebook when that happened, but this phenomena has moved from strength to strength thanks to its' ease of use, with 50 million Facebookers increasing to 150 million in the year from June 2007 to June 2008.

This is one of the reasons why Obama decimated McCain, thanks to the wonders of the internet age and social networking. Barack's team included the co-founders and CEOs of Google and Facebook. He gets this tech stuff. That's one of the reasons why he could raise so much and gain such loyalty.

Could the same be true of new payments providers, who see the EU opportunities and decimate the traditional banks by doing so?

In this era of mass collaboration, fast moving connectivity, innovative entrepreneurialism, where is our engagement in these capabilities in our PSD and SEPA worlds? Where is our incorporation of authorities, institutions, corporations, individuals and observers in our development and deployment of SDDs and SCTs? Where is our critical mass going to come from, if we don't open this to all?

Alternatively, we can keep this as a bank-owned project with no end-date and no demand – and become irrelevant.

What I mean by irrelevant here is that we do literally become just plumbers and pipes.

For those of us in business or at home, do we worry about who gets rid of our water and how? Not really. As long as it works, it's fine.

In banking and the supply chain, do we worry about who processes our payments? Not really. As long as it works, it's fine.

That's what I mean by being irrelevant.

To be relevant, we must start focusing upon the demands of customers, and the innovations we can deliver to them through SEPA instruments, products and services. I know some banks are doing this, but we have to do this in collaboration with our customers, not in these isolated, back office silos. Start creating some really strong client propositions that are client engaged, client tested and client demanded for SEPA instruments. Then we'll really have something to go with, and might even be able to compete with the fleet of foot new competitors such as PayPal.

So what is the cost benefit of SEPA? (2007)

Strange how two subjects get to dominate discussions – SEPA and MiFID – and I promise to move on shortly but, after yesterday's European Council vote to approve the Payment Services

Directive (PSD) and Charlie McCreevy's doomsday warnings about failing to transpose MiFID in time, I guess my recent rantings about both of these Directives are coming to a close.

However, I think it worth one brief, final pause to look at the cost-benefit of these things.

For a while now, we've estimated MiFID's costs as anything from £1 billion to £50 billion ... the fact is that no-one knows although the FSA's views should be taken as pretty reliable, and they conclude that for the UK "the quantified one-off cost of implementing MiFID could be between £870 million and £1 billion with ongoing costs of around an extra £100 million a year." My guess would be therefore about three times that amount for Europe, although my own figures still top-load this with the knock-on business process and related changes.

Anyways, that's not the focus today but to continue with yesterday's news which reminded me of a number of interesting reports and discussions around the cost of SEPA.

There was the 74-page RBR report commissioned by the European Commission in 2005. This one looked at Regulation 2560/2001, which establishes the principle of equality of charges for domestic and cross-border payments within the Eurozone. The Regulation has applied to ATM cash withdrawals and purchases by payment card since July 2002 and to credit transfers since July 2003.

Conclusion?

"This study has found only limited evidence of price increases since the implementation of Regulation 2560/2001."

In fact, the real bottom line of the study is that banks if anything are bringing in differential pricing to encourage customers away from high cost processing payment instruments – cash and cheques – and move them over to efficient instruments – electronic and self-service online.

There is also the 123-page document released with the PSD's draft in December 2005 which goes through a number of figures and issues. The critical costs and issues being summarised as:

The high cost of the payment system to the economy due to inefficient use – the payment system allows for the successful conclusion of 231 billion payments per year in the EU representing a total value of €52 trillion. Studies estimate the cost impact of the payment system to society to be as much as 2–3% of GDP. Cash is the main cost driver and accounts for as much as 60–70% of the total cost of the payment system. Instead of efficient electronic payment services, for which the costs range between a few euro cents the cost per transaction when paid for in cash ranges between €0.30 to €0.55.

Deficiencies in EU payment infrastructures and services where infrastructure for payments in the EU is predominantly national. These national payment systems have not yet adapted to fit the Single Market. Cross-border payments amount to only 3% of total transactions and common technical standards and business rules are missing to allow for competition between national payments systems and cross-border payment systems. The lack of standards also prevents consolidation of payment systems and the redundancy of systems creates higher costs for providers, users and the economy.

Large differences in the efficiency of payment services in the Single Market where, despite the fact that the Single Market exists since 1992, the Internal Market for payment services is hugely fragmented. Whilst it is difficult to compare efficiencies of national markets, the figures that do exist show substantial differences. The price of providing basic payment services related to a bank account varies between Member States by a factor of 1:82, e.g. from €34 a year for the average customer in the Netherlands to €252 in Italy. It is not only on price that large differences are seen between Member States. For example, in some Member States payments are executed in real time or same day, but in others three days or even longer is the rule.

Lack of efficient competition and a level playing field in the payments market in that the payment industry is a network industry and a certain degree of co-operation between competitors is necessary (e.g. to establish common standards) in order for the system to function efficiently. However, the Commission received many complaints from new market entrants from the nonbank sector, about substantial barriers to entry to the payments market and an unlevel playing field. New players are often faced with difficulties when trying to join existing national payment systems and infrastructures, which are a prerequisite in order to be able to compete.

Fragmented legal framework for payment services means that efficient national payment services and systems are not available on a cross-border basis due to legal and technical barriers. For instance direct debits which are a common and cost-efficient service to pay for utilities are not available for payments in different countries. Similarly most of the popular and cheap national direct debit cards are not operating across borders. As illustrated by these fundamental problems the current state of the EU payments market is unsatisfactory.

Now I make no apology for cutting and pasting all that stuff out of the report, and I've already written about the pros and cons of this a while ago, but the main reason I repeat all this stuff is to remind that there is a point to this. No matter how much we scream, squeal, shout, rant and rave about Brussels, SEPA, McCreevy, MiFID and all the other stuff, there is a point ...

To make Europe efficient ... to allow Europe to compete with the USA and China ... to ensure we have an efficient, well-functioning financial system with single infrastructures for clearing, settlement, trading and investing on a pan-European basis.

164

That's why yesterday's agreement is believed to have saved European citizens at least €28 billion a year and possibly as much as €100 billion. So, having one system across Europe rather than one in every member state of Europe must be good for competition and service, mustn't it?

Chapter 6 Fraud and security matters

Introduction

Of course, when you make a payment you want to ensure that it is you making that payment, and not some nutter who stole all of your credit cards going on a retail jamboree. This is why fraud and security matters, although banks know that it only matters so much. In fact, there is an 'acceptable' level of loss built into the system, as you can never eradicate the criminal element in payments completely. You just try to minimise their ability to access and operate. So fraud and security is all about identifying legitimate payments, protecting the bank and their customers from illegitimate payments, and catching the rogues who are trying to steal your identity.

Why identity management is so complicated (2010)

It fascinates me when we talk about 'identity' that we always seem to think of identity management as being a single thing ... but it's not. First, there's the use of identity for identification; second for authentication; third, for verification; and fourth for fulfilment.

Then there are the many instances of providing and proving identification: at a bank, at an airport or border control, at a vehicle hire firm or other high cost rental, when opening a telephone account or similar service, when picking up tickets for a concert, etc.

Finally, there are the many reasons for needing identity checks, from tracking money laundering and politically exposed persons (PEPs) to fraud and identity theft issues to just checking that you are who you say you are.

Although these all sound the same, they have distinct differences and is the reason why there are so many identity solutions out there. Generally, such solutions fall into a catchment of being for an anti-fraud focus or for a verification process, with the process being based upon:

- Something you know, such as a PIN, password or personal fact;

- Something you have, such as card, token or telephone;

- Something you are, such as a fingerprint, voice or other biometric;

- Somewhere you are, based upon GPS location or similar proximity analysis;

- Some way you behave, such as your general activities, channel usage and location.

Obviously the five areas above are also inter-connected, as you could use a PIN, biometric and telephone along with location services to verify a user based upon five-factor authentication rather than two. But we don't do that today, and some banks struggle with even one-factor authentication.

You cannot be serious, I hear you cry, but no, it's true.

Ring your bank and pretend to be someone else. I've done it. I had to pretend to be my father-in-law and it was easy once you got the bravado together to claim to be someone you're not.

So the question of identity for authentication and verification is still not good enough.

What are the potential solutions out there? Generally, further variations on the above.

For example, I recently went to a presentation by a number of firms that use the words identity in their company name. Both firms were focused upon improving password security by offering easier password access and control. I then got a call from another firm with identity in their name, and they wanted to talk to me about biometrics. A third firm offered to provide mobile-based authentication services.

So let's look at these variations in a little more depth.

First, the something we have. This is the most basic form of identification – a document, validated by an authority, that says: "yes, it's you". Often a card and sometimes a card with your photograph on it, this identification has been around since the war. The trouble with this form of identity is that it can be forged, copied, stolen and easily used by another card holder.

Therefore, we introduced the something you know. The idea here is that there is a secret code that goes with the card to show that not only is the person presenting the card the owner, but they can prove it. The most common something you know is a Personal Identification Code, or PIN. PINs are generally allocated by the bank but can be changed to whatever you want. Although secure therefore, it's easy to second guess or, due to chip & PIN, shoulder-surf and steal.

Equally, PINs can be hacked and compromised via intelligent machine-in-the-middle attacks and so banks introduced a four-digit PIN password enhancement by asking things like date of birth and mother's maiden name.

It soon became obvious that criminals could find out such information from public record and so we are now in a world of much more complex codes and secrets.

For example, GrIDsure offer a pattern-based PIN so that criminals cannot predict your PIN numbers. Equally, RSA security offer lots of tokens and keys to generate one-time passwords on top of basic identity information, to ensure that a criminal is foiled.

Unfortunately, in the latter case, many of these efforts just add to the effort required for the customer every time they are trying to make a payment or access the bank service. For example, we have the Chip Authentication Program (CAP) and Personal Card Readers (PCR) in the UK for online payments processing.

The trouble is that you have to have the terminals with you and, even if you do, people use them so infrequently that they often forget the process. As a result, their use of online payments falls, whilst PayPal goes from strength to strength.

The reason?

PayPal is simple, easy and convenient, but PCRs are not.

Equally, what is really interesting in the two instances above, is that these things are already being side-tracked by the mobile telephone, which offers something you have that is unique – your SIM card and telephone number – along with an interactive dialogue for access to PINs and One-Time Passwords.

In addition, it offers an easy way to track where you are, and hence can be a good way of triangulating information for a bank. For example, if someone tries to withdraw cash or make a payment in New York when their mobile telephone GPS signal is being picked up in San Francisco, the bank could immediately question such transactions.

Therefore, I wholly expect the mobile telephone to become the key to most forms of identification.

The mobile can even play directly into the biometrics field, thanks to fingerprint recognition and even apps under discussion that will use the mobile telephone's camera for iris or face recognition. In particular, the work of Voice Commerce to create voice biometric payments is of interest here.

Voice Commerce is now a PSD-approved Payments Institution and Visa Partner, all based upon mobile voice biometric services.

So where does that take us?

The mobile telephone becomes the unique identity management system for future financial services? Sure, it provides a clear capability to track behaviour and location, along with easy verification and validation of something you have and something you know and potentially something you are.

But is that it?

What happens if you lost the telephone? What happens if you forget the codes or passwords? Is voice biometrics really ready for prime time? What I am really asking is: what is the process on the other end of the telephone that's required?

This still therefore mandates a clear bank identity management system, shared across multiple institutions, which can allow the user to access finance with just a single sign-on rather than multiple sign-ons.

That's the thought for next generation financial services. A simple multi-bank, cross-border identity system that can work easily and simply and conveniently behind the mobile bank interface.

Hmmmm ... I wonder what system that could be?

Whichever system it is has to have a number of key features.

First, it will not just be a technology solution, as there must be clear and recognised policy, legal and operational rules which allow the scheme to operate across borders and banks.

Second, an identity scheme cannot just be a "number". Numbers are too easy to break, and you therefore must have a name specified and associated with the number in order for the identity management system to allow transactions to be truly non-repudiable, as in legal.

Third, solutions have to be massively scalable, which means cloud-based today.

Fourth, it must be capable of supporting multiple applications across multiple geographies and multiple industry silos.

And, whilst achieving all of the above, it needs to be simple to use but unbreakable.

Now that's not so difficult, is it?

Chip & PIN is broken (2010)

As many readers know, I've disliked chip & PIN pretty much since it was launched, as there are better solutions out there. Now, just to add insult to injury, Steven Murdoch discusses how they've cracked chip & PIN on Finextra, and references a 13-page research paper which explains how it works:

"EMV is the dominant protocol used for smart card payments worldwide, with over 730 million cards in circulation. Known to bank customers as 'chip & PIN', it is used in Europe; it is being introduced in Canada; and there is pressure from banks to introduce it in the USA too. EMV secures credit and debit card transactions by authenticating both the card and the customer presenting it through a combination of cryptographic authentication codes, digital signatures, and the entry of a PIN.

"In this paper we describe and demonstrate a protocol flaw which allows criminals to use a genuine card to make a payment without knowing the card's PIN, and to remain undetected even when the merchant has an online connection to the banking network. The fraudster performs a man-in-the-middle attack to trick the terminal into believing the PIN verified correctly, while telling the issuing bank that no PIN was entered at all.

"The paper considers how the flaws arose, why they remained unknown despite EMV's wide deployment for the best part of a decade, and how they might be fixed. Because we have found and validated a practical attack against the core functionality of EMV, we conclude that the protocol is broken.

"This failure is significant in the field of protocol design, and also has important public policy implications, in light of growing reports of fraud on stolen EMV cards. Frequently, banks deny such fraud victims a refund, asserting that a card cannot be used without the correct PIN, and concluding that the customer must be grossly negligent or lying. Our attack can explain a number of these cases, and exposes the need for further research to bridge the gap between the theoretical and practical security of bank payment systems."

Update, 13 February 2010

The UK Cards Association dismissed the claim, saying that while the research had shown what it was possible to do in theory, this did not mean it was practical or even possible to do in reality.

A spokeswoman said: "We believe that this complicated method will never present a real threat to our customers' cards. It requires possession of a customer's card and unfortunately there are much simpler ways to commit fraud under these circumstances at much less risk to the criminal. This fraud is also detectable by the industry's systems."

She added that figures due to be released by the group shortly would show that fraud committed on lost or stolen cards during 2009 had fallen to its lowest level for two decades.

Eye, eye – the future of customer identity? (2010)

After the news of a banker's offspring trying to blow up a flight on Christmas Eve by hiding explosive materials in his underpants, we wonder how such individuals get away with such acts. Can't we monitor them better? Is there no way to identify the honest person from the dishonest from the outright terrorist?

This is a core issue in all aspects of modern life, and particularly in banking where it is wrapped up in our AML and KYC rules. On the one hand, we want to give customers good service which should be helped by knowing the client; on the other, we want to avoid dishonest or politically-exposed customers, which is why we have such rigorous account opening and transaction reporting standards. But are they that rigorous?

9/11 was funded by hundreds of sub-$1,000 transactions, and a person who keeps a straight line until the day they walk across it is hard to pre-identity. This is why we need to identify customers better in the future, and to avoid the lapses that account numbering systems expose us to. For example, we are meant to have a standard bank identification code for accounts across Europe in the form of IBAN and BIC, and yet the identifiers vary from 15 to 31 digits so there is no standard. Equally, there are no unique identifiers, in that I could have multiple accounts in multiple names or variations of a name: Chris Skinner, CM Skinner, Christopher Skinner.

This is why banks have been at the forefront of working with technologies that should help identity customers better and more easily and, today, the security services in the airports might provide answers for bankers' dilemmas over customer recognition and identification.

For example, for years banks have investigated biometrics as part of the solution to identity issues. Fingerprints and, more recently, iris-recognition ATMs, palm-print ATMs and facial scanners have been trialled at many banks worldwide. What these systems should deliver is instant recognition of anyone anywhere.

But we are a long way away from such solutions. For example, in my own travels, the number of times my ATM card is rejected in foreign climates on the basis of a 'standard security check' is becoming a common occurrence. Each time, it involves a telephone call to unlock the card, and this simple example shows just how far we are from finding viable method today of secure identification.

Sure, a telephone call seems fairly trivial in avoiding a potential fraud, but the customer inconvenience in both time and cost – a long-distance call to the bank is expensive – is intrusive and unwarranted for a world where technology has solved most other issues of convenience and access.

175

By way of illustration, almost a decade ago Steven Spielberg presented a vision of 21st century life in the film 'Minority Report', where everyone was known by the blink of their eyes. Although the film was released in 2002, the vision of simple iris recognition is still far away from our reality – if you have tried such services at airports, you will know what I mean – but the effective and unique recognition of individuals is a key tenet of banking.

We need a unique single identifier of the individual, and something that can be easily used and presented anywhere, anytime by the individual, and fit for the second decade of the 21st century.

This does not mean a pure biometric recognition but, by adding a biometric recognition to an account at least it may overcome the clunky, chunky way we currently recognise customers through complex numbering systems and passwords that customer's often forget.

And biometrics has become an area that is far more sophisticated than the ropey systems of a decade ago. For example, over a third of ATMs are based upon biometrics using palm vein authentication in Japan in 2008, and the number has been increasing rapidly to avoid fraud.

Or take the use of facial recognition systems in China. These were deployed extensively for the Beijing Olympics, with facial recognition chosen as the way to go because they are completely unobtrusive. These were accurate to the point of false positives or negatives only occurring on a rare occasion, with the ability to search over a million faces in under three seconds on a standard PC.

Now that's simple.

What this shows is that banks and financial markets do have viable alternative customer recognition systems that are far more unique to the individual than an account number, password and PIN.

Using fingerprints on a mobile phone for example. Using fingerprints on a mobile phone, palm-prints at an ATM or facial recognition within branches all add an extra layer of security for a bank to uniquely identify the customer quickly and easily.

The real danger is that banks are no longer in the driving seat when it comes to customer identifiers ... governments are as they impose citizen identifiers.

Citizens are increasingly expecting biometrics to be imposed upon them by governments and until banks start to work with the security services on these programs, the danger will be that they end up having to use whatever the governments give them.

And that might just be something that works well in tracking pantsbombers, but will be incredibly onerous and anti-customer for a bank user.

Forget payments, think value (2009)

When I began talking to banks many moons ago, everyone referred to payments as "money transmissions". Money transmissions were the core service of the bank. Money transmissions were payments, and money transmissions locked customers into the bank because of their high frequency and regular contact with the customer. Money transmissions were the ultimate banking service and ruled the roost.

Over time, money transmissions evolved into payments processing and now transaction services. It became less important as other areas, such as investment banking, became profitable and gained favour.

Nevertheless, payments and everything about payments is very much back in vogue as a reliable source of revenue and profitability.

There's a problem with this, however, as the whole thing is still very much geared towards the same focal point of moving information about money between people and businesses. This is still the heart of banking. The thing is that the heart is being transplanted as we speak, and few seem to be noticing the change.

This only occurred to me recently when I realised that the reason we cannot get rid of cash is that it is a physical manifestation of value. To steal my cash, you have to physically take it from me. To steal my money transmissions, however, you only need to access the data involved in the transmission.

Once you get hold of a 16-digit card number, combined with a valid name and address, you can raid someone's account as much as you want. This is why we are so wrapped up in securing our data, and believe that by adding CVC numbers – another 3 or 4 digit secure code – and PINs to the card details, we can protect ourselves and our customers from fraud.

But this is missing the point. The point is that we focus upon transmission, payment and the exchange of data about money.

But we do not need to think this way, and it certainly is not the customer's focus. Customers don't think about exchanging money. They think about exchanging value. You have something of value that I need – goods and services – and I have something of value that you need – which might be money, but could just as easily be air miles, labour, time, prizes ... you name it.

You see, value can take many forms. Value can be points collected in air miles or loyalty programmes. And value can be the ability to gain access to areas that are inaccessible, such as a backstage pass to a Beyoncé concert. And value can have different levels of value depending upon your view. For example, I believe that a backstage Beyoncé pass has far more value than a backstage Britney Spears pass. However, a Britney Spears fan would say the value of the latter is way beyond the former.

In fact, if we start thinking about value exchanges instead of monetary exchanges, we can start to think differently. We can think about eBay as a value exchange for goods and services priced at the point of value for the buyer. But the buyer is not paying with money for goods – rather, they are setting a value on the meaning of the goods to their life. This is why some may pay $1,000s for a backstage pass to a Liza Minnelli concert when most of us would pay $1,000s not to have one.

Banks could re-engineer their business to be far wider, deeper and meaningful if they dropped the idea of money and replaced the thinking with value.

Banks as a safehold for value and valuable items. Banks as a transaction service for exchanging value between buyers and sellers. Banks as a secure processor of global value.

Maybe it's semantics or maybe it's not, for a value exchange moves the remit of a bank to be far more than just a transmitter of data about money. It means the bank can be a transmitter of data about anything. A bank could be a transmitter of ideas, patents, music, books, documents ... anything.

Aha, you might say, but isn't that what the internet does?

Absolutely, but the internet does this without any guarantee of security. This is why financial infrastructures are so important, building their businesses upon such secure foundations. Secure transmissions of data about payments.

But some are changing that remit. For example, I remember SWIFT releasing their 2010 vision back in 2006 with the following statement from the then CEO, Lenny Schrank:

> "You don't change visions too often, but for 2010, we're considering modifying one word. Although it's still work in progress, we might change 'messaging' to 'transaction management' or 'business process management'. That is profound and deep. Many of our members have transaction businesses. We think we can move up the value chain from offering just

messaging to offering messaging with transaction management services."

It's also what the European Payments Council is doing with SEPA, as things like e-invoicing have related to, but is not actually part of the bank's processing for making payments. Sure, it's affiliated, but e-invoicing is far more to do with the secure transmission of data about goods and services.

Maybe this is why I'm thinking we need to get away from thinking about money as part of the financial transmissions process now. Instead of money transmissions, it's secure transmissions of things that hold value.

Interesting.

I wonder what new products and services a bank could unleash as a secure transactor of value.

We know who you are ... or do we? (2009)

Talking about knowing where and who the customer is, I attended a fascinating discussion earlier in the week. We were brainstorming security, trust and protection of critical financial infrastructures and had a variety of breakout groups looking at different aspects of such systems.

The breakout group I joined started with a scenario of the near future. The scenario stated that: "the European Commission agrees standards for user-centric identity management standards" and the group facilitator asked for our thoughts.

It seemed innocuous enough to me, so I expected a five minute chat about how that seemed like an obvious thing to do and move on. But no, this scenario caused a great deal of debate amongst the financiers in the room that lasted over an hour!

Here are a few select thoughts and comments from the four bankers who I've called Alfred, Bert, Charlie and David.

Alfred: What is "user-centric"?

Bert: The user manages their own identity rather than some central control.

Alfred: Can consumers be trusted to manage their own identity when they give everything away on Facebook, Bebo, etc?

Bert: What's the alternative?

Alfred: Net-centric identity management, with everything controlled centrally.

Charlie: That's no good if the user gets locked out though.

David: But the issue is not about stealing someone's identity. You're still you whatever happens, so you still have your identity. The issue is someone copying your identity.

Bert: That's why net centric doesn't work because someone can easily steal bits and bytes of identity data.

Alfred: Yes, this is why user centric doesn't work either.

Charlie: What about biometrics? That's a way to maintain a unique identity isn't it?

Alfred: Not really. Biometric identity management is also just bits and bytes of data that can be compromised and copied.

David: Sure, but that's why we need the government to be involved here, as they have a role to give a legal context to identities.

Alfred: So who manages identity? The user, the government or someone else?

David: Not a bank then?

(General guffawing in the room.)

Alfred: What about federated identities?

Bert: I'm not sure that works as you cannot have multiple identities. That's the issue we have today. And, coming back to your point about who manages identity, it should be the user as they are closest to their own identity. Therefore, if we are concerned about people giving that data away, we need to educate and incentivise users to manage their identity better.

David: It's not about identity; it's about proving your identity with something. That something is based upon knowledge (a PIN, maiden name, password) and/or a token (card, mobile, chip).

Bert: How about a mobile telephone with a biometric reader in the phone, combined with an account number, PIN and password. Surely you're getting towards an unbreakable system that way?

Alfred: I could break that just by knowing that data. The data is harder to get but it wouldn't stop me.

Charlie: But is our concern identity or the fraud that comes from compromising identity and, if the latter, it's not so great that it should cause us concern.

David: What's not so great?

Charlie: Fraud losses. I'm more concerned about credit losses.

Alfred: Yet if identity is compromised it can lead to massive loss.

Bert: Sure, and net centric and government controlled identities are all easily compromised. I mean every time I check into a hotel they get a copy of my passport along with all my credit card data. Similarly, some stores ask for photo identity and can steal my credit card and driving licence information at the checkout. So how easy is all that?

David: Again, let's clarify what we're talking about here. A credit card is just a number that provides an access right to a financial transaction, right? It's an access right but it's not an identity, ok? The access right is proof of who you are and what we're saying is that this is no longer sufficient.

Charlie: That's a big point. It's not identity itself but proof of identity that we need to focus upon.

Bert: And today it's not enough because we give our access right data at systems all over the world using American operating systems, Chinese hardware and Israeli security software, and so there's plenty of holes in the architecture that can be compromised.

Alfred: The key is to have a safe and secure electronic data stream to manage identity as all identifiers are translated into data. And so it went on, and on, and on, and on ...

... unbelievable how complex this identity stuff can get isn't it?

How many cards are left in chip & PIN terminals every day? (2008)

The banking industry continually seeks to find cost-effective methods to minimise fraud, although often in a way that creates issues or insecurities with the customer. A great example is the UK's implementation of chip & PIN, with Canada, France and other countries implementing similar programs. The reason it is a good example is because:

◆ There is a really cheap (passive terminal) and slightly less cheap (dynamic terminal) version of chip & PIN – the UK implemented the really cheap version which is easier to hack;

◆ It took a long time to implement chip & PIN – a five-year decision to rollout cycle – by which time, there were better technologies around to authenticate; and

◆ The exposure of PINs in public places has not been positive, with many people finding their PINs being stolen due to shoulder-surfers or through dodgy staff at petrol stations.

On the other hand, it has had some success, with fraud moving to Cardholder Not Present (CNP) targets, such as the internet.

In the latest thoughts on this, APACS commented on card fraud post-chip & PIN, and finds that fraud abroad is highest in the USA (£24.6m) and Italy (£9.6m), because both countries operate without chip & PIN. For example, UK cards fraud in France "decreased by £4.3million in two years, and France has dropped to fourth place for where fraud on our cards is committed ... (as) a direct result of the French introducing the same global chip & PIN system that we are using in the UK."

Yowzah!

Congrats to the chip & PIN Fraud Team. Except that there are still too many cracks in the framework.

On the one hand are major stores, such as Tesco, which have yet to fully implement the technologies; on the other, are multiple stories about chip & PIN security regularly being compromised.

From a personal perspective, the one thing I have noticed is that consumers continually leave their cards in the terminal. On four occasions this month, I've found someone else's card left in the POS PIN terminal. People just forget to take the card out after entering their PIN. Silly folks.

The last time I found someone's VISA card, I asked the shop assistant how often it happened and they said at least three or four times a day. That was at just one PIN terminal in one major store, so I wonder how many cards are left in terminals each day?

The solution? An audible message when you enter your PIN saying "please take your card". So simple, but so easy to forget.

Meanwhile, the real bottom-line is that by the time we rolled out chip & PIN, other methods of cutting out card crime including mobile telephone alerts, dynamic security keys and biometrics, had become available. The challenge now is how to incorporate these methods, which appear to be more secure and affordable, when so much has been invested in chip & PIN.

This house believes our authentication and identification methods work (2008)

Last night's debate, "This house believes our current authentication and identification methods are good enough", was a healthy one and focused primarily upon card authentication in retail transactions.

We started with the case for. The motion was proposed by one of the major card processing firms, who said that the card firms are trying to do more than enough to protect cardholders. They talked about the Chip Authentication Protocol (CAP), a method of making card present even when remote by asking the cardholder to use a calculator style terminal to authenticate.

This program has just been rolled out in the UK and means that each time you make an online payment, you enter your PIN plus a special one-time system generated code into a special card reading terminal.

In addition 3D secure, the pop-up window where you enter a unique and personal password for a transaction, provides an additional layer of security, as do the use of IP addresses and other location-aware services. Combine this with chip & PIN and all the other ways in which we are protecting cardholders, and our current authentication and identification systems are good enough.

This view was refuted by a representative of one of the credit reference agencies, who claimed that authentication goes further than just card protection and must look at the process for client account opening. This process is subjected to rules for AML and KYC which are clearly flawed, as they are totally reliant upon paper. These paper-based processes are easily subjected to fraudulent activity because utility bills, driving licences and even passports are easily forged.

Back to the proposal and the UK's leading payments authority made it clear that we are doing what we can with what we have.

Governments are responsible for issuing identities – passports and driving licences – and we need better management of this part of the process. In other words, the identity card systems are not within our control, and we can only use systems that are within our control.

Given this constraint the industry has achieved a lot and, where we have control, it works. In fact, where it is within our control, we go as far as we need to go in order to satisfy our appetite for risk. The whole authentication process therefore is built around acceptable levels of risk.

Finally, the representative of a firm that provides remote identity confirmation determined that the views of both proposers were flawed. Chip & PIN had had a little success when first introduced, but was proving to be broken already as the systems is regularly undermined by petrol station attendants.

The CAP reader is a good idea, but means that anyone who gets our card, PIN and CAP reader can now spend excessively online too, making our online purchasing protection even more compromised.

Meanwhile, 3D Secure is a neat idea, but only 10 million of the UK's 140 million card users have signed up for it, which shows it is not that great. In other words, for all the efforts of the industry, the customer is not buying into our authentication processes and therefore they must be flawed.

Following these open gambits, with the proposers saying that we've done what we need to do and the opposers retorting that it's not enough, the floor was open for debate.

Points were raised, such as the fact that claiming identity management is the government's job is a cop-out, isn't it? Waiting for the government to issue ID cards will be a long wait, and surely the industry should do some work beforehand?

There were questions about the speed of change, and why the industry takes so long to implement and improve processes. For example, with mobile and biometric authentication available, why are we not implementing these systems?

The answer was that the industry can only move as fast as its slowest players, which is not necessarily the banks, but the merchants and retailers who must also be brought on board. Many of these retailers are SMEs and mid-caps, and so embracing all UK business in the process is a key barrier to speed of change.

Surely customers also have some responsibility for their own protection of identity. The fact that customers expect the industry to make them secure, without taking any responsibility themselves, is just ludicrous.

But customers only like security when it's convenient, which is why CAP and 3D Secure are proving tough to make a success. 30 percent of UK consumers are abandoning online payments due to the inconvenience of CAP for example.

Is there a point at which we move from customers being idiots and responsible for their own protection versus the industry being at fault, because we should have educated the customer to be more responsible?

The evening wound its course to conclusion, with the conclusion being 'the motion': This house believes our current authentication and identification methods are good enough.

All those in favour? 27%.

All those against? 63%

The motion is rejected.

PINs and passwords: useful or useless? (2008)

On the day of the first anniversary of chip & PIN, which happened to be Valentine's Day, I was quoted in one newspaper as saying chip & PIN is completely useless. Not the best way to endear yourself to the banking community but, in retrospect, not far off the truth. Why?

Because it's only secure for as long as the PIN is secure. The chip is fine. It's just the PIN that's useless.

Think about it as being like your most secure password. In fact, there are some close analogies between PINs and passwords. For example, think about your online banking password. Now then, what happens with that password? According to most surveys, you use the same one everywhere.

For example, a survey by Get Safe Online finds that over half of UK internet users use the same password for more than one website and 17% use personal information about themselves in passwords, which opens them up to all sorts of easy hacking options. You know, the hacker sits there and thinks: "I know his middle names are James Murgatoyd, so let's try Murgatoyd ... wow, it worked".

Now the importance of Get Safe Online is that it is an initiative combining the efforts of the UK government, the police, HSBC, BT, eBay, Microsoft and SecureTrading. Their report, which can be found at http://www.getsafeonline.org/media/GSO_Cyber_Report_2006.pdf, has a range of highlights including:

Do you use the internet for:

Online banking	52%
Paying utility bills	32%
Buying insurance	29%
Completing tax return	11%
Arranging a loan	11%

Which of the following do you feel most at risk from in your everyday life?

	2006	2005
Bank card fraud	27%	40%
Burglary	16%	18%
Internet crime	21%	17%
Mugging	11%	13%
Car theft	8%	10%

24% have been deterred from internet banking

21% won't do their financial management online

18% won't shop online

17% have been put off using the internet all together

83% have virus protection, compared to 80% in 2005

78% have a firewall, compared to 75% in 2005

20% hadn't updated their virus protection in the last month

23% had opened an e-mail attachment from an unknown source.

My favourite figure in this report was the fact that only 24% of people think they should be primarily responsible for their own online safety. In other words, 76% think they're not responsible for their own safety when shopping, banking or doing stuff on-line? They must be nuts. After all, it's their PC, their keyboard and their system that is exposed – no-one else's. So why should it be someone else's fault if they get defrauded online?

Anyways, back to the point which is that folks are not that bright. Ask them to use a password and most of them – over half – will use the same password for everything. Ask them to use a different one, or to change it every month and never use the same one twice, and what do they do? They write it down on a post-it note and stick it on their PC or the top drawer of the desk.

So, passwords are not secure. That's why we're trying so many other ways of introducing online security through random number generators and other things.

Which brings me back to PINs, and chip & PINs greatest advocate: APACS, the UK Payments Association.

APACS has lots of good stuff on their websites about secure payments, including advice on shopping online. For example, their website www.cardwatch.org.uk provides these top tips for safe web shopping:

- ◆ Sign up with Verified by Visa or MasterCard SecureCode;

- ◆ Don't give away your PIN or password to cold callers or in response to unsolicited emails;

- ◆ Use a computer protected by up-to-date anti-virus software and a firewall;

- ◆ Keep your cards and card details safe when you are shopping in the real world as most internet fraud happens because card details are stolen in the real world and then used online;

- ◆ Only shop at secure websites and make sure that the security icon – the locked padlock or unbroken key symbol – is showing at the bottom of the browser window before sending your card details. Also check that the beginning of the retailer's website changes from http://

to https:// when a purchase is being made with a secure connection;

- ◆ Make sure your browser is set to the highest level of security notification and monitoring;

- ◆ Always check your bank statements. If you find a transaction on your statement that you did not make, contact your bank or card company immediately;

- ◆ Destroy, or preferably shred, any documents that contain information relating to your financial affairs;

- ◆ Use one credit card specifically for internet transactions so you can monitor transactions at a glance;

- ◆ When shopping online make sure you get a hard copy of both your order form and the retailer's terms and conditions.

In particular, the comment about looking for https:// and the padlock is interesting as I've recently started asking folks: "do you look for this every time you shop online?" and, strangely enough, I haven't found anyone yet who does this religiously, including yours truly if I'm honest. As I said, folks ain't that bright …

Anyways, APACS have loads of research and other good stuff about the internet, cards, fraud and advice.

So why did I copy all of this advice here, apart from the fact it's worthwhile reading?

I'll tell you. APACS introduced chip & PIN to the UK in 2004 and made it mandatory from 14th February 2006. They've talked about how great it is, how it's working and how it's made fraud and theft a thing of the past. And I agree with them. It is a good programme. It has reduced fraud. It works. So please don't get me wrong here. It's not APACS I'm having a go at, or the idea of having a bit of added security.

Money for Nothing and your Cheques for Free

I mean, the fact that chip & PIN has reduced card fraud significantly must be a good thing. According to APACS, chip & PIN helped to reduce card fraud by 24% in 2005, saving us all about £60 million.

Today, the chip & PIN figures are quite impressive with:

- 99.9 per cent of all chip & PIN card transactions now PIN-verified;
- 185 chip & PIN transactions being processed every second (125 a year ago);
- 97% (138 million) of all UK cards chip & PIN enabled; and
- 98% (900,000) of all shop tills upgraded to chip & PIN.

That's great. Cost us about £1.1 billion and is saving £60 million a year. So far, so good.

I should mention that we followed other countries that had success with chip & PIN, so it was a proven model. For example, France, Netherlands, Austria, Belgium and other countries experienced the same gains, with many of these countries operating over 90% of payments verified by PIN. In fact, the success is spreading worldwide with Canada introducing chip & PIN this year and it can only be a matter of time before the USA and rest of the world follow suit.

Fantastic. Chip & PIN works.

Now, finally, to the reason I said chip & PIN is useless .In the APACS advice for online shopping, two of the top tips are:

- Don't give away your PIN or password to cold callers or in response to unsolicited emails;
- Keep your cards and card details safe when you are shopping in the real world, as most internet fraud happens because card details are stolen in the real world and then used online.

OK, this is the bit that conflicts with chip & PIN. You see, I hate PIN. It's one of those things where, when you're standing at the merchant's terminal, you feel completely naked don't you?

Maybe some of you are naked depending upon what you're buying, but my PIN is the only security I have to protect me from rampaging hoards of criminals who will steal all my money.

That's what my bank has drilled into me for years and I learned the message: don't let anyone know anything about your PIN. Don't ever breathe the PIN code. Don't write it down. And, if anyone ever finds out your PIN, jump off the nearest tall building ... or call your bank, whichever is easier.

I got the message. PIN is Fort Knox for consumers.

So when APACS advise me to keep my PIN secret, don't tell anyone about it, and keep your card details safe in the real world ... why the hell am I tapping my PIN number for all to see every time I buy something in the real world?

And my PIN happens to also be regularly used in my passwords by the way. After all, when you're forced to put in "secret word" and the website says "your secret word needs some numbers too", guess which numbers we use? Yep, nine times out of 10 we use our PIN.

So, chip & PIN completely contradicts what I thought the PIN was for, as in a secret code you only ever used discreetly. That is why we now have "shoulder-surfers" – the folks who look over your shoulder in stores to see your PIN number. That is why many stores now have signs saying "Please do not stand too near to the person at the till" so that you don't see their PIN number being entered. This is why Shell petrol stations have a yellow line on the floor. Not because it's pretty, but so that they can put up a sign that says "Please stand behind the yellow line so that you do not see the PIN number of the person at the till".

Wow, this is so safe and secure isn't it?

In fact, it is why the BBC has been on the case of chip & PIN for sometime, and recently ran a programme about how banks are now blaming customers for losses if their card is used fraudulently

Money for Nothing and your Cheques for Free

as "you must have told the fraudster your PIN number mustn't you, so it's your fault, you dumb schmuck."

APACS spokesperson Sandra Quinn countered these accusations by saying "Chip & PIN was never going to eradicate fraud, but our cards are certainly much safer because of it. Decreasing card fraud figures prove this. Most critically, any innocent customer who is the victim of this or any other type of card fraud, is protected by the Banking Code, which means that they will not lose out financially"

Mmmmmm … this is going to be a long debate. Nevertheless, I agree with some of what Sandra says. Chip & PIN has made it significantly more difficult for a fraudster to use a lost, stolen card or a counterfeit card in the UK. In fact, it's pushed people to start doing fraud in other ways, for example, online. That is why Card Not Present (CDP) fraud rose 21% in 2005, as internet, phone and mail order fraud increased by £32.4 million. Typical isn't it? Chip & PIN helps to reduce fraud by 24% in 2005, £60 million, so the fraudsters just move elsewhere.

And another thing: why did we do chip & PIN so late? France and the Netherlands did chip & PIN in the early 1990s, and the UK finally gets there in 2005. What happened, and weren't there alternatives?

There were. Just that we went with chip & PIN just as others were thinking about chip and biometric or something else. What is interesting though, is that I raised this question about why were we so late in getting to chip & PIN with a bunch of senior anti-fraud leaders. The discussion went something like as follows:

Head of Fraud #1: "Chip & PIN is a classic example of how the banking industry sat on its hands in this country for years. If you look at what had happened in France, there was good evidence that proved that technology worked but the investment was very long in coming through in the UK. By the time we got there, we're in a position where the criminals are moving on and have made other plans."

Head of Fraud #2: "Yes, but the only real visionary investment the UK has made, rightly or wrongly, is chip & PIN. Everything else has been tactical."

Head of Fraud #1: "We should have done chip & PIN years before, as the French did, but I guess the business case simply wasn't there."

Head of Fraud #3: "If we had gone looking for something else at that time, would there have been any suppliers or technology people playing in that space?"

Head of Fraud #2: "I think there was or is stuff out there, but chip & PIN was implemented on the basis that everything would be offline."

In other words, in the typical speed at which risk-averse financial firms move, we took years to make a decision to do something. When we finally made a decision it then took a few more years to implement it and, by the time it was all done, everyone had moved to shopping in a different way such as online.

That's why, in the first six months of 2006, UK online fraud increased 55% to £22.5 million, which provides an all-up estimate of £60 million for they year – about the same amount we saved in 2005 by moving to chip & PIN.

Final thoughts here and then I'll stop my rant.

If chip & PIN is so good, why are we thinking of other ways to protect the poor defrauded consumer? For example, there are two new systems already being considered as an add-on to chip & PIN.

One is produced by Gridsure (http://www.gridsure.com/). These guys overlay a pattern based approach so that, even if someone knew your pattern they couldn't work out your PIN number. Another is Swivel (http://www.swivelsecure.com/) which you can see in action by going to the Bank of Adelaide, http://www.adelaidebank.com.au/, and clicking on the 'login here' picture.

What both of these systems are doing is trying to ensure you do not actually enter your PIN number, but you enter something else that correlates with your PIN number such as substituted numbers of words. This way, no keylogger or shoulder-surfer gets to see your PIN, just a randomly generated code.

The key question for all of us though is to ask: "if chip & PIN was that good, why do we need these additional systems?" My answer is that it is because chip & PIN is not that good. But, once again, don't get me wrong. It is not the chip that's at fault. It's the PIN. Therefore, I do have a solution. After all, if chip & PIN is useless then the over £1 billion UK stores and banks have spent on this program is a little bit of a waste isn't it.

My solution is that chip will always be critical to payments. Therefore the chip reading infrastructures we have implemented are a worthwhile investment and will be used for the long term by retailers, merchants and banks.

Chips are the payments mechanism for the 21st century. Chips in phones, in cards, in jewellery and watches and inside people. Chips are key.

Therefore, we will stick with our crude chip & PIN in 2007, but gradually move towards chip and patterns, such as Gridsure or Swivel. Shortly thereafter, we will maybe use chip and biometric, such as fingerprints, palm-prints or, ideally, signatures. Yep, a biometric signature. Now then, returning to signatures – what a radical idea?

Eventually, as we all now know from the example of the Baja Beach Nightclub in Spain, we'll get to chip-in-skin.

Whatever we use, it is only the authentication that changes though. The infrastructures for biometric chips and patterns are the investments we have now made and therefore, although there may be additional costs, it will be incremental rather than completely different.

Chips. Chips are the future, not PINs. PIN is just our chunky, clunky out-of-date method to authenticate chips securely ...

... blimey, I think I've said so much you could hear a PIN drop?!

Chip and PIN five years from now (2009)

So I finally sussed out a way to make my long-term vision of sticking chips inside people for payments a reality through a medium-term transition away from my short-term loathing for chip & PIN.

This will be achieved as we strip things back to the basics.

For example, look at any credit card today and it's got a chip on it (unless you're in the US where mag stripe still rules). That chip is the EMV – Europay, Mastercard, Visa – chip and is capable of basic functionalities, including intelligence to be used with payments terminals with a PIN.

The thing is, why do you need the card bit?

I mean, you have a payments card with a chip ... why do we need the plastic holder for that chip? Because it has a mag stripe? Duh ... that one went out with chip & PIN. Because ATMs have big slots to put cards in? Yeah ... today. Because payments terminals have big slots to put cards in? Yeah ... today.

So in the near, medium-term future, this will all change won't it?

What got me to thinking about this is that I'm totally in love with the Kingmax USB stick I carry around in my wallet. It's tiny, flat, and is the smallest USB flash drive in the world. It is so small that it is almost the size of a paper clip. It is not only small but also very thin, because it's basically a USB device stripped down to the basic chip. Throw away all the plastic bits and that's all you're left with – the chippey connections.

That's all you need isn't it?

A little like flash memory for digital cameras and mobile phones that started as those credit card sized sticks and are now the size of fingernails, with double, triple, quadruple the memory, everything is getting stripped down to basics.

Except credit and debit cards. They're still HUGE. So why not throw away all those plastickey bits on the cards and cut it down to the basic chip. Ahh ... 'cos we'd then have to throw away all of our ATMs and card terminals.

Shame. And not true. You're just switching the card slots to a chip slot or a contactless communicator. And here's the upside. A basic, standardised bank chip could be multi-bank, multi-application, stored value holders. When you get to paying, it could have all your financial providers' details – not just one bank's, but all of them – and you could then just pick the icon of the card processor you want to use for that transaction.

Equally, if we standardised the chip to something like a USB or flash memory drive, then we could use that chip as a direct chip insert into PCs and mobile telephones.

This leads to the chip & PIN vision of five years away.

Five years away, you have a pure, standardised bank chip that can be inserted into any PC, mobile, payments terminal or ATM, in the same way as a bank card. You only have one chip, and the plastic bit has gone. Effectively, your bank chip is just the chippey bit you currently use on your credit card. And that chip is powerful with 10Gb, 100Gb, 1Tb (Terabyte) storage and even some dumb intelligence built-in, so you could do almost anything with it.

It could be multi-bank and multi-function, wirelessly enabled and communicating. It's contactless, cashless, debit and credit payments in home or local currency – you name it. Most of the time, for low value transactions, it asks for no authentication but now and then it wants ID. You then enter either a PIN, provide a biometric or other agreed verification. Away you go.

Now, you're concerned that if the chippey bit is that small, then you'll lose it. But no, because you can stick that chip into anything. You might hold that chip in your wallet, mobile telephone, watch, ear-ring ... you could even stick it up your wherever if you wanted (now that could be a safe harbour).

That's the short-term future of cards as they become chips.

Bring it on.

Lightning Source UK Ltd.
Milton Keynes UK
31 January 2011

166665UK00001B/172/P